Augsburg Commentary
on the New Testament
I, II, III JOHN

Robert Kysar

Augsburg Publishing House

Minneapolis, Minnesota

AUGSBURG COMMENTARY ON THE NEW TESTAMENT
1, 2, 3 John

Library of Congress Cataloging-in-Publication Data

Kysar, Robert.
  1, 2, 3 JOHN.

  (Augsburg commentary on the New Testament)
  Bibliography: p.
  1. Bible. N.T. Epistles of John—Commentaries.
I. Title.   II. Title: First, Second, Third John.
III. Series.
BS2805.3.K87   1986   227′.94   86-17416
ISBN 0-8066-8862-9

Manufactured in the U.S.A.   APH 10-9044

1   2   3   4   5   6   7   8   9   0   1   2   3   4   5   6   7   8   9

To Kathy and Karen
"Perfect Love Casts Out Fear"
(1 John 4:18)

CONTENTS

Foreword 7
Abbreviations 9
Introduction 11

1 John 25
  Outline   27
  Commentary   30

2 John 119
  Outline   121
  Commentary   122

3 John 135
  Outline   137
  Commentary   138

Notes 149
Selected Bibliography 155
About the Author 159

FOREWORD

The AUGSBURG COMMENTARY ON THE NEW TESTA-
MENT is written for laypeople, students, and pastors. Laypeople
will use it as a resource for Bible study at home and at church.
Students and instructors will read it to probe the basic message
of the books of the New Testament. And pastors will find it to
be a valuable aid for sermon and lesson preparation.

The plan of each commentary is designed to enhance its use-
fulness. The Introduction presents a topical overview of the biblical book to be discussed and provides information on the historical circumstances in which that book was written. It may also
contain a summary of the biblical writer's thought. In the body
of the commentary, the interpreter sets forth in brief compass
the meaning of the biblical text. The procedure is to explain the
text section by section. Care has also been taken to avoid the
heavy use of technical terms. Because the readers of the commentary will have their Bibles at hand, the biblical text itself has
not been printed out. In general, the editors recommend the use
of the Revised Standard Version of the Bible.

The authors of this commentary series are professors at sem-
inaries and universities and are themselves ordained. They have
been selected both because of their expertise and because they
worship in the same congregations as the people for whom they
are writing. In elucidating the text of Scripture, therefore, they

attest to their belief that central to the faith and life of the church of God is the Word of God.

The Editorial Committee

Roy A. Harrisville
Luther Northwestern Theological Seminary
St. Paul, Minnesota

Jack Dean Kingsbury
Union Theological Seminary
Richmond, Virginia

Gerhard A. Krodel
Lutheran Theological Seminary
Gettysburg, Pennsylvania

ABBREVIATIONS

LXX   The Septuagint (the Greek Old Testament)

NT   New Testament

OT   Old Testament

1QS   *Manual of Discipline* from the Qumran writings (the Dead Sea Scrolls)

RSV   The Revised Standard Version

SBL   Society of Biblical Literature

TEV   Today's English Version

INTRODUCTION

No other document of the NT speaks more often and more explicitly of love than does 1 John, and for that reason alone it has become dear to the hearts of many Christians. Aside from this one claim to fame, however, the so-called "Epistles of John" stand in the shadow of the gospel which is called by the same name and are lost among those minor writings referred to as "the Catholic Epistles." Still, they present us with expressions of the life of the earliest church in the throes of a struggle for unity and integrity, and for that reason alone merit study.

This introduction will treat the three writings together, although their differences will not be ignored. The task at hand is to investigate four topics important to their interpretation: (1) authorship, (2) literary nature, (3) the situation, and (4) theological message.

1. The Authorship of the Epistles

None of the epistles identifies its author by name. The first has no mention of the author, while the second and third declare themselves to be from the hand of one who calls himself "the elder" (*ho presbyteros,* 2 John 1 and 3 John 1). Consequently, their identification with one another under the name of John arises, not from explicit evidence within the writings, but from traditional association. Their further identification with the Gospel of John is also traditional, although it has a good basis, as we shall see below.[1]

The question of authorship involves two interrelated problems, both of which are fraught with difficulties. The first is whether or not the three epistles are from the same author, and the second concerns the relationship of the author(s) of these writings to that of the Gospel of John.

With regard to the first question, the only thing that can be said with confidence is that 2 and 3 John each claim to be written by "the elder." Given that, we may assume that they share a common authorship. But their brevity makes it difficult to assess the relationship of their authorship with that of the first epistle. Linguistic and stylistic arguments falter, due to the fact that there simply is too little evidence for a comparison with 1 John. Moreover, as we shall argue below, the literary nature of 2 and 3 John is different from that of 1 John. The latter is clearly not an epistle in the strict sense, as are 2 and 3 John. We do find, however, some common uses of words and concepts among the three (e.g., "truth," 1 John 3:18; 2 John 1-4; and 3 John 3-4). Between 1 and 2 John we find other similarities, such as the use of "abide in" (e.g., 1 John 2:28 and 2 John 9). But the evidence is too meager to allow a firm conclusion.

In favor of a common authorship it may be argued that all three epistles betray concerns from what might have been a common situation. First John is clearly directed toward a community torn apart by schism (e.g., 2:19) which, at least in part (e.g., 4:2-3), resulted from doctrinal disputes. Second John likewise reflects an interest in those who hold a doctrinal position contrary to that of the author, and it is the same theological issue which surfaces in 1 John, namely, the humanity of Jesus (v. 7). In 3 John there is evidence of disruption in the community, but in this case it is not clearly a theological matter that is at stake. It is rather that one rebellious leader of a congregation has refused hospitality to others and rejected the authority of the author (vv. 9-10). The common concern of 1 and 2 John suggests the possibility of a common author, and the fact that 3 John is also concerned with dissenters in the church may also be used to argue the same point. But again the evidence is inconclusive at best (cf. §4 below).

The most that can be said with some assurance is that the three epistles reflect comparable situations and that they share some common language and conceptuality. It may be that they were written by persons who shared a common tradition—and perhaps life—in the same community. The "elder" responsible for 2 and 3 John may be the same person who wrote 1 John, but proof of such is beyond our reach.

Is the fourth evangelist responsible for one or more of the epistles traditionally attributed to him? Contemporary scholars are divided over this question, much as were their counterparts of the fourth century. Again, in the case of 2 and 3 John arguments are hampered by the sheer lack of data. Stylistic and linguistic evidence is, therefore, of little use. One can, however, point to some common words and themes as evidence for common authorship.[2]

The evidence is most impressive when the gospel and the first epistle are compared. Even a hasty reading of the two reveals a good deal of common language and themes. For instance, the expression "abide in," prominent in the gospel (e.g., 15:5), appears no less than 11 times in 1 John. "Eternal life," a favorite expression of the fourth evangelist (e.g., 3:16), can be found in 1 John six times, and the simple "life," which in the gospel is used as a kind of abbreviation for "eternal life" (e.g., 1:4), appears five times in 1 John. Other expressions found in 1 John which are familiar to the reader of the gospel include "world," "light/ darkness," "Spirit of truth," and the use of "Son" as a title for Jesus. Such evidence of a common set of theological themes and vocabulary is the most impressive argument for a common authorship of the gospel and first epistle (cf. note 2).

However, evidence for different authorship can be drawn in a similar way. Terms important in the gospel are missing in the first epistle, such as "glory," "glorification," and "sign." On the other hand, 1 John is filled with concepts which are not found in the Fourth Gospel and seem even contradictory to its theology, e.g., the imminent "last hour" (2:18), "expiation" (2:1 and 4:10) and "antichrist[s]" (2:18, 22; 4:3).[3] The weight of this evidence seems almost to offset that cited above.

Other evidence against the proposal that the author of the first epistle was the fourth evangelist includes the following: (1) Difference in style between the two documents;[4] (2) the absence of OT quotations in the epistle and their abundance in the gospel; (3) the proposed Hellenistic character of the thought of 1 John when compared to that of the gospel (e.g., it has been proposed that "God is Spirit" in John 4:24 is consistent with Jewish thought, while the equation of God with "light" in 1 John 1:5 and "love" in 4:8 has a more Hellenistic flavor); and (4) the fact that the author of 1 John seems familiar with sayings of Jesus found in the Synoptic Gospels but not in the Fourth Gospel (e.g., compare Matt 7:15, 20 and 24:11 with 1 John 4:1; cf. Dodd, pp. xxxviii–xli).

Thus, the evidence for a common authorship of the gospel and the first epistle seems weak, and the evidence against it strong enough to commend caution. Indeed, the data suggest that, rather than being from the hand of the same person, the two documents arose from the same *community*, but stem from two different authors at two different periods in the history of that community. This suggestion explains at the same time both the similarities and the differences between the two writings.

When we compare 2 and 3 John with the Gospel of John, the hope for finding a common author dims even more. To be sure, there are some common themes among the three (cf. note 2). For instance, the "Father-Son" language, used so frequently in the gospel, occurs in 2 John 3, 9. But beyond that there is little to be said in the support of common authorship. To the contrary, a considerable number of themes in 2 and 3 John are missing in the Fourth Gospel, and may even be at odds with the theology of that book. Examples are the use of the word "church" in 3 John (6, 9, 10) and the reference to the congregation as a "lady" in 2 John (1, 5; cf. note 3). It is best to conclude, then, that 2 and 3 John were probably not written by the fourth evangelist.

However, if 2 and 3 John are to be linked with 1 John (cf. note 1), it may be that they, too, are from the hand of one who shared with the fourth evangelist the same community. If so, they, like 1 John, are also reflections of the same community at another point in its history, even though they are not from the same author. Our proposal, in summary, is that the epistles are products of and for a Christian church that shared a tradition embraced by the author of the Fourth Gospel. Time has passed, and the circumstances of the community are much different from those at the time of the writing of the gospel. But the gospel and its author are part of the heritage of the church reflected in the epistles.

The feasibility of this hypothesis will be demonstrated further when we discuss the situation out of which the epistles were written (§3 below).

2. The Literary Nature of the Epistles

While these three writings are commonly called "epistles," the label is not appropriate in the case of 1 John. Clearly 2 and 3 John are in the form of letters—the first to a congregation or congregations identified only as "the elect lady and her children" (cf. commentary below) and the latter to an individual, Gaius (cf. Brown, *Epistles*, Appendix V, for a discussion of the epistolary form). About their literary form there can be little doubt.

The literary genre of 1 John, however, is another matter. It has persistently puzzled scholars in their efforts to classify it, and indeed it would seem to represent a form unique to the NT. It lacks those features by which we have come to identify an ancient letter. For instance, there is neither a salutation nor a conclusion. Its internal order suggests nothing of the kind of "conversation" we often find exhibited in the NT epistles, e.g., 1 Corinthians (cf. the outline of 1 John, below).

Proposals have run the gamut. It has been labeled a "circular or general epistle," suggesting that it was written to be passed among a number of churches. For some it appears to be a tractate, for others a homily or pastoral statement (cf. Smalley, who calls it a "paper," p. xxxiii). Still others see it as a contemporary interpretation of the Gospel of John for the author's community. None of these suggestions is entirely satisfactory, for a number of reasons.

Upon examination it appears that 1 John is comprised of fragments of messages having to do with a range of topics, perhaps all of which relate to a crisis of division within a Christian community. Its lack of clear order and structure points to the likelihood that its present form is the result of a hurried union of disparate pieces. The easiest and simplest way of making sense of its literary form is to view it as a kind of anthology of bits of sermons patched together and rendered into a written form for circulation. We might imagine a leader of the community drawing together paragraphs delivered on a number of different occasions into one short document. The frequent use of expressions such as "I am writing" or "I write" (e.g., 2:1, 7, 8, 12, 13, 14, 21, 26; 5:13) represents an effort to give the document the appearance of a letter. The purpose of such an endeavor would be to produce in writing what had been said with regard to a number of issues relevant to a somewhat broader audience. If this proposal is sound, we can further imagine that the product was then passed about to those who were affected by the current situation of the community. The nearest comparison in NT literature would be Hebrews. But the literary form then suggests the further question of the situation of the community that would provoke such a writing.

3. The Situation of the Epistles

In each of the three epistles there is reference to dissenters who, in the opinion of the authors, represent threats to the life of the Christian community. If anything binds these three documents together, it is their polemic character; each attacks an opponent of some sort.

In 1 John we gain the clearest picture of the author's opponents. Four explicit charges are leveled against them: First, it appears that they do not exercise love in relationship to the other members of the Christian community (2:9-11; 4:20-21). Second, they have separated themselves from the community (2:19). Third, they do not acknowledge the humanity of Christ (4:2-3), which leads the author to say that they do not accept the Son (2:23). Fourth, they are "of the world" and the "world listens to them," as opposed to the true believers (4:5-6). The seriousness with which the author views the position of the dissenters is expressed in the fact that he speaks of them as antichrists (2:18-23) and, by implication, as the devil (3:8).

From this sketchy picture we conclude that the dissenters in the case of 1 John were a group of Johannine Christians who believed that Christ was not fully human and who for one reason or the other did not practice love toward those who held different positions. This led eventually to their withdrawal from the community. Scholars have often seen a resemblance between this description and the tendencies of "gnostic Christians," who are often called "docetists," because they held that Christ only appeared (Greek, *dokeō*) to be human when in fact he was pure spirit. Furthermore, the group the author describes compares to the "antinomians" among the gnostics who taught that the Christian was free of all moral law—in this case the commandment to love other believers (John 13:34). The author even accuses the opponents of "lawlessness" (3:4). While we do not want to suppose that these dissenters are full-blown gnostic Christians such as arose in the second and third centuries, they appear to have been separatists who held positions which anticipated the emergence of gnostic Christianity.[5]

In 2 John the "docetic" feature of the dissenters is reaffirmed. The author speaks of "deceivers . . . who will not acknowledge the coming of Jesus Christ in the flesh" (v. 7). The wording is nearly the same as that of 1 John 4:2. Like the author of 1 John, the elder views his opponents' position with grim seriousness and calls them "the deceiver and the antichrist" (v. 7).

In 3 John, however, the situation is quite different. The complaint the elder has against his opponent is not a theological one at all. Diotrephes is accused of four things: First, he "likes to put himself first" (v. 9a). Second, he has refused to accept the authority of the elder and gossips about him (vv. 9b-10). Third, he has refused to welcome "the brethren" (v. 10). Finally, he has dismissed from the church those who had disagreed with him (v. 10). Here we see evidence of the clash of two church leaders. Diotrephes seems to have been a leader of a local congregation, while the elder saw himself as an overseer of a number of congregations within a certain region, whose authority (he asserts) is greater than that of the congregational leaders. "The brethren" were probably representatives of the elder, itinerant prophets commissioned by the regional authorities to minister to local congregations. That the elder is disturbed by the dismissal of members who come into conflict with Diotrephes suggests that the elder regards such action as an usurpation of authority on the part of a local leader.[6] The picture we glimpse through the scant words of 3 John is of a rather well-organized structure in the church with clearly defined lines of authority—a picture not unlike that presented in the Pastoral Epistles (e.g., 1 Tim. 3:1-16).

While the opponents of 1 and 2 John are quite different from those described in the third epistle, it is not difficult to imagine them all arising from a similar situation. If we are to hold 3 John together with the first two epistles, it would appear that a basically theological and ethical conflict has become in the case of Diotrephes, a conflict of authority. Diotrephes may have been one with dissenting tendencies who has rebelled against the authority of the elder, or he may have been a local leader confused by the entire situation and unsure of whom he could trust. In any case, the basic issue seems to have been one of Christology and ethics which (like so many theological disputes in the church) gave rise to disruption in the authority structure within the organization of the community.

The image of the church in the epistles is, then, that of a community torn into at least two major factions and struggling for its continued existence. If our analysis of 3 John is sound, the community consisted of a number of congregations within a single region which looked to one centralized group for its leadership— a parent church with satellite congregations. Both the developed church structure suggested by 3 John and the nature of the theological-ethical dispute implied in 1 and 2 John point in the direction of a late first-century date.

Our earlier conclusions supposed that this body of Christians embraced as part of their tradition the Gospel of John and the community for which it was written. A comparison of the situation out of which the Fourth Gospel came with that we have proposed for the epistles gives us some idea of the changes in the Johannine community between the time of writing of the gospel and that of the epistles. (For a description of the proposed situation of the gospel cf. Kysar, *John*, Introduction.) The focus of conflict for the community has switched from relationships with the synagogue (gospel) to relationships among its own members (epistles). What was an external conflict has become an internal one. The structural freedom of the church inferred from the gospel has given way to a rather refined organization of authority. The relative isolation of the Johannine community from other churches, which seems to have prevailed at the time of the writing of the gospel, has been replaced with some sense of the larger Christian body. The differences in the theological teachings of the Fourth Gospel and the epistles may be due to the fact that by the time of the writing of the epistles the Johannine community had adopted the views of the "mainstream" of Christian thought in the latter half of the first century (cf. §4 below). The authors of the epistles seem clearly to be moving away from the uniqueness of the theology of the Fourth Gospel toward a stance within the emerging "normative Christianity" of the time. These changes would seem to require at least a decade, which means that the epistles may have been written A.D. 90–100 (supposing a date of 80–90 for the gospel).[7]

The task of the authors of the epistles was to defend the parent body of Christians against the threat of the separatists. This necessitated that, insofar as possible, the separatists be shown wrong in their beliefs. This accounts for the radically defensive quality of 1 and 2 John. The readers must be assured that their position is true and consistent with the faith which came to them from their tradition (meaning, at least in part, consistent with the Gospel of John). The lines of distinction between the separatist and the parent body must be sharply drawn, leaving no doubt as to the difference between them. A community in schism is a deeply threatened community, fearful for its existence, uncertain of its identity, defensive and angry. The order of the group must be preserved at all costs, and so it is natural that the lines of authority should be strengthened and emphasized, as is attempted in 3 John.[8]

4. The Theological Message of the Epistles

The situation which called forth the writing of the epistles shapes the theology expressed therein. The most important contributions of the epistles to NT thought center in two areas: Christology and morality.

Central to the theological message of the epistles is the insistence that the Christ (God's messianic agent) be identified with the human, Jesus of Nazareth. This insistence arose as a response to the danger in the position of the separatists, which seems to have been ready to compromise that identification in order to preserve the divine, spiritual nature of Christ. First John asserts that *Jesus* is the Christ (e.g., 4:15; 5:1). Both 1 and 2 John declare that the appearance of the Christ was "in the flesh" (*en sarki*, 1 John 4:2 and 2 John 7), an expression surely reminiscent of John 1:14 and meant to invoke the tradition of the community's faith. First John 5:6 probably intends to assert the full humanity of Jesus ("water and blood"), again in the tradition of the Gospel of John (19:34). "Water only" in the same verse may represent the separatists' view that there was only a temporary association of Christ with the human Jesus in his baptism.

This Christological stance is given status as the true faith—faith now conceived of as proper doctrine or creed. "Doctrine" (*didachē*, literally, "teaching") in 2 John 9-11 is what defines proper faith. Around Christology there has developed a distinction between true and proper teachings—a step toward the emergence of an orthodox position. With that step may have come a corollary, namely, the emerging authority of the elder of the community in 3 John.

Connected with the Christology of the epistles is the soteriology of 1 John—its view of the death of Jesus as an atoning expiation for sin. Unlike the Gospel of John, which never clearly articulates a sacrificial view of the cross in cultic terms, the author of the first epistle proffers the view that Jesus' death was an "expiation" (*hilasmos*, 2:2; 4:10). In this sense, the death of Christ is understood as an offering to God for sin, with the possible connotations of an appeasement of the divine for human wrong. In that context, too, the author can speak of Jesus' blood as a "cleansing" and a "taking away" of sin (1 John 1:7; 3:5). It is clear that this author has come under the influence of non-Johannine views of the cross, and employed those views to reinforce his argument for the morality of Christian life.

The second major contribution of the Johannine Epistles to theology lies in the area of morality. The necessity of the moral life arises out of the situation in which the church found itself, much as does the Christology of the epistles. Over against a view which seems to have disregarded moral injunctions, the author of 1 John stresses the absolute centrality of the righteous life. He condemns "lawlessness" (*anomia*), and equates sin and the absence of law (3:4). He also attacks the position which claims that the Christian is free of sin (1:8, 10). This suggests that his opponents' claim of freedom from the law is bolstered by their confidence that they are without sin. But, at the same time, the author of 1 John asserts that the Christian does not sin (3:6, 9).

These contradictory positions with regard to sin in the life of the Christian are confusing at best. It may well be that the contradiction arises from the fact that two different homiletical fragments, which have been combined in the Epistle, make two different points, each having been uprooted out of its original context (now lost to us). It may also be that there are two concepts of perfectionism represented in the two sets of passages. On the one hand, a Johannine perfectionism recognizes that unbelief is the only sin and that the Christian, by virtue of her or his faith, is by definition sinless. Such a view could have been rooted in the Gospel of John, where sin is understood primarily in terms of unbelief (e.g., 15:22-24; 16:9). The perfectionism the author is attacking in the insistence that Christians cannot claim to be free of sin is one that is at home in a gnostic framework. Those who belong to God (the true God) are created without sin, and those who are sinful are the responsibility of another, minor deity. The author's concern for those who are "born of God" (2:29; 3:9; 4:7; 5:4, 18) shows that he is trying to counter the views of the separatists by insisting that affiliation with God does not mean one is freed of moral obligation. The author, according to this "situational" explanation of the contradiction, would be posing a Johannine perfectionism over against an antinominiam one (cf. Bogart).

In the first epistle's concept of sin we find another important, though—for some—questionable, contribution. In 1 John 5:16-17 there is a distinction between mortal and nonmortal sin. This distinction seems to arise from the author's conviction that all wrongdoing is sin, but that some has a more serious consequence than others. "Mortal sin" is for this author unbelief or false belief, while "nonmortal sin" is the wrongdoing within the context of faith. Those who do not believe that Jesus is the Christ are bound to a sin whose consequence is mortal—death. This arises out of the view of the Gospel of John, cited above, that sin essentially is unbelief. He is concerned, however, to take that view and develop it in a context of Christian ethics (a concern the fourth evangelist did not have), and hence he suggests a kind of sin (nonmortal) which is the result of human failure to live out the imperatives of the Christian commitment.

The moral imperative is, therefore, an absolute for the writer of 1 John. If the commitment of Christians is genuine, they will not walk in "darkness" but do the righteous thing and keep God's commandments (1:6; 2:29; and 3:7). To be "born of God" (e.g., 3:9), to be "children of God" (e.g., 3:1), to "abide" in God (e.g., 2:6) or Christ (e.g., 2:24) or the light (2:10) are all expressed in, or made evident by, righteous living.

In this connection we encounter the centrality of love in the epistles. Love (*agapē*) is the nature of God and of his act in Christ (4:7-12), and since God has loved us, love is the character of the Christian life. Christians are exhorted to love one another because God has loved them (4:7-12), to love others because it is the commandment of God (3:14), and to love in deed as well as in word (3:18). We cannot love God and at the same time fail to love other humans (4:20). The love imperative is the certain consequence of receiving God's love and loving God in return. For this author there is no conceivable way by which the indicative of God's love cannot issue forth in the imperative of intrahuman love.

Conclusion

The Johannine Epistles show how the church in the late first century was forced to wrestle with internal differences and conflict. They demonstrate both the necessity for the rise of proper doctrine, to protect the gospel message against misunderstandings and distortion, and also the inescapable need for structures of authority within the church. The church had to define the outer limits of belief and practice, not only to defend itself, but also to maintain its integrity. In many ways, the epistles reflect the Christian community in a real-life situation not unfamiliar to the church of the 20th century.

I JOHN

OUTLINE OF 1 JOHN

Any proposal for the structure of 1 John is tentative and inadequate, for the document defies efforts to render its order logical. This is due to the simple fact that logic, as we understand it, did not seem to be a high priority for the author. Instead, the style of the document is semipoetic, moving from subject to subject more under the control of free association than careful structure of thought. Modern criteria of logic falter in the face of this kind of order.

Still, the structure of the document possesses a kind of power in its own right. The outline proposed below attempts to express some of that power, especially by highlighting such characteristics as the following: First, the major parts of the document are dialectical in their nature. That is, each part poses two topics and explores the interrelationship between them. This feature is expressed in the titles of the major parts in the outline below. Second, each major part (after the first, 1:5—2:11) is connected with the preceding by a word or concept association. These are noted in parenthetical comments accompanying the major headings. Third, each of the major parts is comprised of three subparts, showing a symmetry within the homiletical fragments incorporated into the book (cf. Introduction §2 above).

I.   Introduction: The Life and Fellowship (1:1-4)

    A. The Experience and Proclamation of Life (1:1-2)
    B. The Resultant Fellowship (1:3)
    C. The Resultant Joy (1:4)

1 John

II. Light and Darkness (1:5—2:11)

    A. God's Light and Humans' Light (1:5-7)
    B. Sin and Its Cure (1:8—2:6)
    C. The Light of the New Commandment (2:7-11)

III. The Believers and the World (2:12-17)
    ("Walks in darkness," 2:11, connects with "sin," 2:12.)

    A. The Victory of Believers (2:12-14)
    B. The Nature and Destiny of the World (2:15-17)
    C. The Passing World and the Abiding Believer (2:17)

IV. Truth and Lie (2:18-29)
    ("World passes away," 2:17, connects with "last hour," 2:18.)

    A. The Antichrists (2:18-23)
    B. Protection from the Lie (2:24-27)
    C. Confidence for the End (2:28-29)

V. Children of God and Children of the Devil (3:1-24)
    ("Born of God," 2:29, connects with "children of God," 3:1.)

    A. The Origin and Destiny of the Children of God (3:1-3)
    B. Children of God Love; Children of the Devil Hate (3:4-18)
    C. The Assurance of Keeping God's Commandments (3:19-24)

VI. The Spirit of Truth and the Spirit of Error (4:1-6)
    ("The Spirit," 3:24, connects with "every spirit," 4:1.)

    A. The Necessity to Identify Spirits (4:1)
    B. The Identity of the Spirit of God and of Antichrist (4:2-3)
    C. Being of God and Being of the World (4:4-6)

VII. God's Love and the Believers' Love (4:7—5:5)
    ("We know the spirit of truth," 4:6, connects with "knows God," 4:7.)

A. God's Love Evokes Human Love (4:7-12)
B. Confidence in God's Love (4:13-18)
C. Love among the Children of God (4:19—5:5)

VIII. The Son and the Witness(es) (5:6-12)
("Jesus . . . the Son of God," 5:5, connects with "Jesus Christ," 5:6.)

    A. The Humanity of Christ (5:6)
    B. Three Witnesses to the Truth (5:7-8)
    C. The Witness of God in the Son (5:9-12)

IX. Knowing and Doing (A Conclusion?) (5:13-21)
("Life" and "Son of God," 5:12, connect with "eternal life" and "Son of God," 5:13.)

    A. The Confidence of Faith (5:13-15)
    B. Doing that Arises from Knowing: An Example (5:16-17)
    C. What the Children of God Know (5:18-21)

COMMENTARY

◼ Introduction: The Life and Fellowship (1:1-4)

The author[9] begins with a confusingly long sentence which runs on for four verses, with the main(?) verb occurring finally in v. 3. The Greek borders on incongruence, represented in the RSV with the dashes between vv. 1 and 2 and vv. 2 and 3. Furthermore, the tenses of the "we" verbs in the first three verses vary indiscriminately between the perfect, aorist, and present. There are no less than 10 of these verbs: "heard," "seen," "looked upon" (v. 1), "saw," "testify," "proclaim" (v. 2), "seen," "heard," "proclaim" (v. 3), and "are writing" (v. 4). Whether our author was careless, rushed, or exceedingly subtle is difficult to say, but his introduction makes for a stylistically awkward beginning.

What is clear from this befuddling array of language is a claim to authority. The repetition of the verbs of experience ("see," "hear," "look upon," and "testify") makes certain to the reader that the author has the prerequisites for speaking out on the subject. The tone is that of one who feels his authority threatened and must somehow lay claim to what he believes is rightfully his.[10]

And what is the subject of this morass? The nominees are: "That which was from the beginning" (v. 1) and "life" (vv. 1 and 2 [twice]), plus "fellowship" (v. 3 [twice]). It would appear that the authority the author claims has to do with that which was in "the beginning" which results in "life" and produces "fellowship." In short, the author claims to know the revelation and desires to share it in order to insure a continuance of fellowship both with God and among believers.

From this introduction the apologetic quality of 1 John is immediately evident. One who asserts authority with such insistence is likely one whose authority has been challenged.

The Experience and Proclamation of Life (1:1-2)

1—That which was from the beginning has several possible meanings: (1) Something that was before time and creation or at creation, (2) the commencement of Jesus' ministry (the beginning of the revelation), (3) the inauguration of the proclamation of the church, or (4) the initiation of the believers' faith. The expression **from the beginning** occurs eight times in 1 John (2:7, 13, 14, 24 [twice]; 3:8, 11, as well as here); **beginning** (*archē*) always occurs with the preposition **from** (*apo*). In a number of passages it is possible to take the expression in the sense of (1) above (2:13, 14; 3:8), but just as frequently it seems to refer to the initial faith of the readers (2:7, 24; 3:11). Thus, our author uses the expression ambiguously to refer variously to the priority of Christ, the gospel, and the readers' initation in faith. That he intended to suggest an ontological status is less clear than that he wanted to appeal to an existential priority for his readers. He wanted to remind his readers of the first importance of the gospel message in the origin of their Christian lives. Therefore, the use of **beginning** by this author is not to be equated with the way the word is employed in John 1:1, although he may have wished to recall that awesome initial statement of the Fourth Gospel.

Here **that which was from the beginning** is the gospel message which the believers embraced in their **beginning** and which roots in the **beginning** which knows neither the limitation of time nor place. Our author can employ words with a subtle ambiguity not unlike (but not nearly as skillful as) his Johannine predecessor, the fourth evangelist.

It is now claimed that that gospel message has been **heard, seen, looked upon,** and **touched.** The verbs are used metaphor-

31

ically to mean that the author has personally experienced the gospel message. The variation in the tenses of the verbs in the Greek seems to be little more than artistic style (or simple carelessness), and sophisticated differences are fruitlessly sought therein. While it might be inferred from these verbs that the author here claims to have been an eyewitness of the historical Jesus, it is more likely that he is appealing to his experience of the gospel in the tradition of the church.

The **we** is problematic, for it may indicate a multiple authorship or may simply be an "editorial *we.*" The alternatives are not really exclusive of one another. The plural suggests that our single author understands himself to be writing on behalf of a community—perhaps the body of leaders determined to maintain their position over against the separatists, whom they regard as distorters of the gospel. Furthermore, the **we** carries the tone of authority—it is the voice of the community of the true faith.

What it is that has been experienced has to do with **the word of life. Word** once again calls to mind the prolog of the Gospel of John (1:1), and that implication is doubtless intentional on the part of the author. But the sense of the word is "message," for there is no evidence elsewhere in the document that *logos* is used with a Christological meaning (cf. 1:10; 2:5, 7, 14; 3:18). With the word **life** however, the author does seem close to the use of the term in the Fourth Gospel, for it is employed here in the sense of the content of the revelation of God in Christ. In v. 2 it is clear that this content was revealed to the author's community. **Life** is both the content and the result of the revelation, insofar as it is the message of the Father's love which makes authentic existence possible. Consequently, the nature of the gospel message spoken of as **that which was from the beginning** is now further explicated—it is a message of authentic existence.

2—That message **was made manifest,** a reference to the revelation of God in Christ. It is not enough to say that the revelation has occurred; the author must further say that it was **manifest *to us,*** repeating the same Greek verb (*phaneroō*). This is one of the frequent verbs in 1 John, occurring nine times (2:19, 28; 3:2

[twice], 5, 8; 4:9; as well as here) variously translated, "manifest," "appear," and "be plain." Again comes the claim to personal experience with the revelation—**we saw it.** It is the message of the revelation to which the author claims to have witnessed in proclamation. Do we have here evidence of the author's appeal to his reputation as a preacher and evangelist to win the confidence of his readers?

In this case, the content of what was manifested is called **eternal life,** a synonym for **life.** The author alternates between these two expressions, using the first six times (2:25; 3:15; 5:11, 13, 20; as well as here) and the second five times (1:1, 2; 3:14; 5:12, 16). That this **life** was **with the father** shows that it is associated with Christ, although it is unnecessary to say that it equates Christ and that **life** is here personalized in the form of Christ (compare John 1:4). **Father** is the favorite Johannine expression for God (cf., e.g., John 5:21); it occurs 12 times in 1 John. It arises from the basic Johannine Father-Son Christology.

The Resultant Fellowship (1:3)

The message the author has experienced is shared with the reader (with repetition of the verbs **seen, hear, proclaim**). The purpose (**so that**) of the sharing is that the readers might be in **fellowship** (*koinōnia*) with the author and those for whom he writes. The consequence of the revelation of life is the creation of a community, sharing in common that divinely manifested gift.

The author's **fellowship,** in turn, **is with the Father and with his Son Jesus Christ.** The gospel message creates a community, not just among humans who share its benefits, but also between humans and the source of the message itself. In the tradition of the Fourth Gospel (e.g., 1:12), 1 John speaks of this community in terms of a family (e.g., 3:1). There is, however, a polemic quality to these words, for they suggest that **fellowship** with the author means **fellowship** with God. If one has broken relationships with the author and those he represents, the implication is that they have forfeited their **fellowship** with God—a point that will be made again in clearer terms (cf. 2:19 below).

The Resultant Joy (1:4)

Finally, the author ends the involved and broken sentence of the first three verses and concludes his beginning with a simple sentence which states the purpose of the writing. **Our joy,** and not "your joy" (see RSV footnote), is the more likely original reading.

The sense of the verse is that in the author's sharing of his convictions his **joy** finds its fulfillment. **Joy** (*chara*) often has the meaning of the eschatological fulfillment in the Gospel of John, and it may well be John 16:24 after which the author has modeled his statement. But in 1 John the word is used only here (cf., however, 2 John 12 and 3 John 4), and it is difficult to ascertain any precise meaning. It is clear that the author feels so strongly about his mission to defend the community and his understanding of the gospel that only in having done so will there be satisfaction for him. **Be complete** (*peplērōmenē*) might be rendered "be fulfilled."

There is a logic to the scramble of these four verses. They first affirm the revelation of God in Christ and then articulate two of the benefits of that revelation—life and joy. It is life which links the revelation and its benefits, for life is both the content of the revelation and its consequence. Joy is the result of sharing the good news of the revelation.

A number of prominent features of 1 John have become evident in its introduction. Already we sense the apologetic quality of the author's style. He must establish his authority in order to accomplish his mission. With some intensity and emotion he lays claim to a firsthand understanding of the tradition he defends. Furthermore, he emphasizes here that it is faithfulness to the tradition which preserves the church from error and disintegration. Only in clinging to "that which was from the beginning" can the community survive the crisis brought on by the recent schism. The author knows the value of a community's history. It is that history, and what has always distinguished the community, which is its principal means of survival in the face of schism.

34

■ Light and Darkness (1:5—2:11)

The first of the major sections of the writing focuses on a contrast which is primarily moral, while taking its origin in a statement concerning God's nature (1:5). The section achieves its unity through its common attention to the quality of Christian life and the references to "darkness" in 1:5 and 2:11. It is comprised roughly of three interrelated themes: God's light and humans' light (1:5-7), sin and its cure (1:8—2:5), and the light of the new commandment (2:6-11). The message of this section is that the believer's life should cohere with the actions of God and that God has provided the means by which this can be realized. This unit is tied to the introduction through reference to **message** (*angelia*, v. 5) and **proclaim** (*apangellomen*, 1:2,3).

God's Light and Humans' Light (1:5-7)

God Is Light (1:5)

5—Message is essentially the same as **word**, used in v. 1; it refers to the content of the revelation. *Angelia* is used only in 1 John (here and 3:11), but the *angel-* words are common NT language for the divine message and its announcement (e.g., Acts 4:2, "proclaiming"; 20:20, "declaring"). The content of the message is expressed in terms of the **light/darkness** imagery. This is both a Johannine image (e.g., John 1:4-5; 8:12; 9:5) and a classical religious symbol. **Light** represents truth, authenticity, and goodness; **darkness** represents falsehood, inauthenticity, and evil.[11] In the OT **light** is often associated with a revelation of God (e.g., Isa. 9:2).

Does the author intend by **light** to define the inner being of God or to express what God is through actions in regard to humans (the essence of God apart from divine acts or the being of God known only through divine acts on humans)? The latter is the sense of the expression in John 4:24. Our author will use a similar kind of formula in 4:8. It is sometimes proposed that he is offering a formulation of the being of God influenced by Hellenism (cf. Dodd, p. lii), but if such is his intent, there is little evidence of it elsewhere in 1 John. It is better to take this as a propositional summary of the kerygma: The effects of God's actions in human history are to demonstrate that God is the source of authenticity for human life. This interpretation is borne out by what the author does with his statement about God, namely, to use it as a basis for discussing the necessity of moral life on the part of humans. Furthermore, that he can say in v. 7 that God "is *in* the light" shows that his statement here is not a strict declaration of the being of God. The Greek of the last phrase (**and in him is no . . .**) is emphatic in its redundancy. (For the expression **in him is,** cf. 2:5 below.)

It is significant, however, that our author summarizes the content of the **message** in terms of a proposition introduced with **that.** If the basic kerygma was an announcement of what God had done in Christ (cf., e.g., Rom. 1:3-4), our author has transformed that historical event into a creedal proposition. This is a reflection of the tendency of the church in the late first century to understand the gospel in terms of propositions—a view which may reflect the influence of Hellenistic modes of thought, but, more significantly, may betray an attempt to draw the perimeters of proper faith and life.

Walking in the Light—Fellowship and Cleansing (1:6-7)

The author begins now a series of five "if . . . then . . ." sentences (vv. 6, 7, 8, 9, 10), in which he explores the meaning of certain kinds of human life-style.

6—The first two "if . . . then . . ." sentences are in contrasting parallelism. Verse 6 is the negative pole of the contrast, while v. 7 is the positive. The former expresses one of the author's favorite themes, namely, the contradiction between confession and life-style. It is formulated in two opposing pairs: **Say** and **walk** in the protasis, and **lie** and **do not live** in the apodosis.

Fellowship (*koinōnia*) is the author's word for the saving relationship between humans and God made possible in Christ (cf.

v. 3 above). It is another form of the more frequent expression "to be in" and "to abide in" (cf. 2:5 and 6 below). **Walk** means to live out one's life in concrete behavior (cf. 1:7; 2:6, 11 below). It is a Johannine expression (e.g., John 8:12; 12:35), and our author's use of it seems modeled after that of the fourth evangelist. But it is also used in Pauline (e.g., Rom. 6:4) and Deutero-Pauline (e.g., Eph. 2:2; Col. 3:7) literature in this metaphorical sense. It is rooted in Hebraic usage (e.g., Ps. 1:1; 15:2). It denotes the specificity of life-style.

Professing a relationship with God while concretely living a life which does not demonstrate that relationship is to **lie** (*pseudomai*). **Lie** carries the significance of disharmony with the truth of the revelation. **Do not live according to the truth** is, literally, "not doing the truth," another expression borrowed from the Gospel of John (e.g., 3:21). "Doing" is another way of referring to the concrete character of life. **Truth** in the Fourth Gospel means the content of the revelation itself (e.g., 14:6), but here in its juxtaposition with **lie** has the simpler sense of integrity.

7—This verse expresses in a positive way what v. 6 has said in a negative way, and completes the contrasting parallelism. The conditional clause (protasis) picks up the image of **walk** from the preceding, and **in the light** refers back to v. 5 and the description of God's relationship to humans. To **walk in the light** is to live out the implications of God's character and actions. **As he is in the light** is surprising, since the author has declared that "God is light" in v. 5 and shows that his language is more poetic than descriptive.

If this condition prevails, two results follow: **fellowship** with other believers and **cleansing.** The words **we have fellowship** in v. 6 were used in reference to a relationship with God; here the same words are used of the common sharing among Christians (cf. v. 3 above). The implication is that a saving relationship with God yields a sense of community among those who share that relationship. But that result, claims our author, comes only where the ethical conclusions of the God relationship are actualized in behavior. The second result is a freeing from the consequences of **sin. Blood, cleanses,** and **sin** suggest a sacrificial understanding of the cross, which the author will make more explicit in 2:2 and 4:10 (cf. below). It is clear that the metaphor of sacrificial worship has been pressed into service to affirm the way in which the death of Jesus relieves humans of the ramifications of their wrongdoing (cf. Rom. 3:25). Such a metaphor roots in the concept of the sin offering in the OT (e.g., Lev. 4:1-12). The NT offers several metaphors for understanding the atoning significance of Jesus' death. It is noteworthy that the Gospel of John never clearly articulates the meaning of Jesus' death by references to the role of sacrifice in the temple worship of Judaism. **Cleanses** means "to free of contamination." **Sin** (*hamartia*) is used by our author in both the singular (as here) and the plural (e.g., 3:5), but in every case the word in 1 John has an ethical dimension, without the cosmic character of Pauline usage (e.g., Rom. 7:11). Sin for our author is the failure to enact in behavior one's relationship with God. **All** expresses the universal effectiveness of Christ's atonement.

The implication of our author's words is that the saving benefits of Jesus' death are appropriated only by proper conduct and character. The cleansing of which he speaks is conditioned by the quality of one's life (**walk**). This is not to say that he knew nothing of a doctrine of grace which makes possible salvation without regard to morality; indeed, 4:19 implies the opposite. But it is the overriding purpose of 1 John to stress the necessity of a morality which issues from the saved relationship with God.

The impact of vv. 5-7 is the inevitable link between the actions of God and a right relationship with God, on the one hand, and human behavior and character, on the other. Furthermore, we witness here the author's strong commitment to a maintenance of the community. Intra-Christian relationship is an essential expression of the relationship of the Christian with God.

Sin and Its Cure (1:8—2:5)
Denial and Confession of Sin (1:8-10)

The promise in v. 7b of a cleansing from sin leads the author to a further discussion of sin and its cure, first by establishing the promise of forgiveness for confessed sin. He employs the third of the series of "if . . . then . . ." sentences, but alters the parallelism he employed in vv. 6-7. Verses 8-10 are each constructed on a pattern comprised of a conditional clause ("If"), followed by a pair of statements joined by "and." The triology of sentences is made up of a positive enclosed by negatives. The structure of the unit appears like this:

> 8—If we say -A, then *a* and *b*.
> 9—If we confess +A, then *c* and *d*.
> 10—If we say -A, then *e* and *f*.

It is important to note that the conditional clauses in each case speak of what humans do and that the statements arising from the conditions in vv. 8 and 10 speak of the results in humans, while the statements from the condition in v. 9 speak of what God does. This puts God's action at the center of the structure (v. 9b). The statements (*a* through *f* in the outline) also betray a certain symmetry: *a* and *b* describe the human conditions if sin is denied (*a*, "we deceive ourselves," and *b*, "the truth is not in us") and *e* and *f* declare the implications for God of the human denial (*e*, "we make him a liar," and *f*, "his word is not in us"). Notice that *a* and *e* are parallel, the first having to do with deceit and the second with lie. Members *b* and *f* are closer parallels: *b*, "the truth is not in us," *f*, "his word is not in us." All of this is to express forcefully and clearly the implications of denial and confession of sin.

8—For **sin** cf. v. 7, above, and v. 10, below. **Deceive** (*planaō*) means to "wander" or "go astray," and our author is concerned with such misdirection and those who cause it (cf. 2:26; 3:7), as is the elder (2 John 7). To deny the reality of **sin** is to "go astray" from a realistic perception of oneself. **And the truth is not in us** is a way of saying the same thing: our self-understanding is false. Given its structure, parallel to v. 10b, however, the expression here may mean that the revelation is absent from the self. **In us** is the author's way of speaking of the relationship between the person and that which determines his or her existence (cf. 2:5,6 below).

In sum, the denial of wrongdoing and alienation reflects a blindness to oneself and a separation from that which is ultimately important in life.

9—Confess is to "acknowledge" or "embrace" or "own" for ourselves (cf. 2:23; 4:2,3,15). The author follows his pattern of using only the pronoun to speak of God (here implicit in the verbal form, *estin*, "he is," cf. vv. 5, 6, and 7). Two adjectives are used to describe God: **faithful** (*pistos*) and **just** (*dikaios*). The former describes God's reliability, consistency, dependability. God can be trusted to do what has been promised. **Just** translates a word which might as well be rendered "righteous," as it is elsewhere in the book in reference to God (2:29). "When said of God [*dikaios*] serves to express that God is always doing what is in accordance with his own will, which is to be good and merciful towards [humans]" (Hass, De Jonge, and Swellengrebel, p. 38). While it does not carry the full theological sense of "the righteousness of God" in Romans (e.g., 3:21), this word affirms that God's actions give expression to divine beneficence.

And is an inadequate translation of the conjunction *hina*. The Greek word implies a causal connection between the adjectives used of God, on the one hand, and God's forgiveness of sin, on the other. "Which is why . . ." might be one way of expressing the association. God's forgiveness flows out of divine faithfulness and righteousness. The Greek verb translated **forgive** suggests that forgiveness is conditioned on the confession of **sin,** and is a singular act rather than a general state. Confession and forgiveness are not once-and-for-all acts but are repeated again and again (however, cf. 2:12 below). **And cleanse us** . . . is synonymous with **and will forgive**. . . . (In this case, the pair of statements following the conditional clause are not strict parallels, as they are in vv. 8 and 10, for the first includes the attributions to God, breaking the tight structure we find in the other verses.) For **cleanse** cf. v. 7 above. **All** suggests again, as in v. 7b, the universal and thorough nature of God's forgiveness. **Unrighteousness** (*adi-*

kias) comes as a variation to the author's use of sin. It is set in contrast to the "righteousness" of God earlier in the verse (*dikaios* vs. *adikia*). (This is another reason for translating the former "righteous" rather than **just**.) For our author, the human lack of righteousness is synonymous with sin, and signifies the failure to enact the righteous actions of God.

10—The last of the five "if . . . then . . ." sentences (vv. 6-10) is parallel to that of v. 8. In the conditional clause, the author uses the verbal form, **sinned,** as opposed to the noun with the verb "have" in v. 8. The difference may be that in the earlier verse attention is given to being of a sinful character, i.e., having a general misorientation in life, whereas here the focus is upon specific acts which betray that misorientation. The verb is in the perfect tense, suggesting an act in the past, the consequences of which still prevail.

The apodosis of the sentence includes two statements concerning the human relationship with God. The first is that God is made a **liar** by the denial of sin. The author uses this word a number of times of humans who either are immoral (e.g., 2:4) or doctrinally wrong (e.g., 2:22). In 5:10 he says that humans make God a liar if they refuse to believe (properly) in Christ. Hence, he holds that humans in effect accuse God of lying when they fail to think correctly about God's act in Christ or to acknowledge their wrongdoing. To make God a liar is to deny who God is and what the divine character is (specifically, God's judging and forgiving actions). Moreover, it is to blur the distinction between God's goodness and the evil of the devil, if the author has in mind John 8:44, since Satan is "a liar and the father of lies." For **word** cf. v. 1. **His word is not in us** means the same as "the truth is not in us" in v. 8 (cf. above). Failure to own our brokenness demonstrates that we have not appropriated the gospel message, which brings with it a conviction of our sinfulness. For **in us** cf. v. 8.

Verses 8-10 express the conviction that God's revelation in Christ demonstrates the sinfulness of the human condition and

God's willingness to correct that condition. Only by affirming the brokenness of their lives do humans avail themselves of that divine restructuring of existence. To deny the brokenness of life is to alienate ourselves from our true being and from the God who would heal us.

The Expiation of Sin (2:1-2)

1—My little children refers to the Christian readers, who are doubtless a part of the author's community. He uses the word *teknion* ("little child") seven times (2:12, 28; 3:7, 18; 4:4; 5:21; and here) in this form of address. The Greek word is the diminutive form of *teknon* ("child"). The author assumes by this form of address a position of spiritual leadership with regard to the readers and an intimacy with them. (For a comparison of the words "children," "little children," and "son," cf. Brown, *Epistles*, pp. 213-214.) Before the author assures the readers of God's act to relieve **sin,** he wants them to know that his intent is to help them avoid such wrongdoing. In contrast to the "we" of the beginning of the section (1:5), the singular first person pronoun, **I,** is used. It seems that the author, when sharing in the witness to the gospel, uses the plural, and, when addressing his readers more personally, the singular (cf., e.g., 2:26).

The transition to the assurance is abrupt. **If any one does sin** sounds strange, given the insistence of 1:8 that all are to acknowledge their **sin. Advocate** translates *paraklētos,* a word used in the Gospel of John for the work of the Spirit (e.g., 15:26, where it is translated "Counselor"). There the Paraclete is given no function in the forgiveness of **sin** (although cf. John 16:9). In this verse the word means "one called to the side of another" for the purposes of defense.[12] For **Father,** cf. 1:2 above. This **advocate** is identified with **Christ,** which is not entirely harmonious with the concept as it is found in the Gospel of John. There the Paraclete is linked closely with Jesus (e.g., 14:16), but the distinction between the two is maintained. In effect, this author assigns the Paraclete a different function and identity from that described in the Fourth Gospel. At best, we can say that the author, or the interpretation of his tradition before him, has taken liberties with the thought of the fourth evangelist. **Christ** is here understood as one who intercedes on behalf of the sinner, as he is said to do elsewhere in the NT (e.g., Rom. 8:34; Heb. 7:25). It is interesting that Paul can say in the same epistle that both the Spirit and Christ intercede for the Christian (Rom. 8:27,34). That same fluidity between the functions of the Spirit and Christ seems to have allowed our author to identify the Paraclete with Christ and give the former the function as an intercessor for sin. **The righteous** (*dikaion*) describes Christ with the same word used of God in 1:9 (cf. there above for the meaning of the word). (The definite article, **the,** is missing in the Greek.)

2—**Expiation** renders the problematic Greek word *hilasmos.* It is found only in this epistle (cf. 4:10), although a number of other words from the same root appear elsewhere (e.g., *hilastērion*, Rom. 3:25, and the verb *hilaskomai,* Heb. 2:17). The basic sense of *hilasmos* is a means of making appeasement, and in the LXX it is used of a sacrificial "covering over" of sin in cultic practices. The basic distinction in the translations, "expiation" and "propitiation," is summarized by Brown: "propitiation is primarily directed toward the offended person, while expiation is directed toward removing what has caused the breakdown" (*Epistles*, p. 219). Clearly, our author has invoked sacrificial imagery to say that the effect of human sin is removed by God's act in Christ. It is unwise to attempt to read into this reference any fully developed doctrine of atonement (cf. 1:7 above). Calling Christ an "expiation" here and an "advocate" in the previous verse, however, gives the impression of a view which understands the cross as some sort of compensation to God for an offense done in human sin. The author explores one way—if a dangerous one—of trying to comprehend the full meaning of the death of Jesus.

The author again affirms the universality of the significance of that death, just as he has insisted that there is forgiveness for "all sin" (1:7) and "all unrighteousness" (1:10). The gift of the cross is not a possession of a single community but is effective for **the whole world,** meaning all humans.

The argument began with the necessity of acknowledging and confessing sin (1:8-10), and has now suggested the way by which God is able to overcome sin. The argument must now move to the question of how humans can know that they have appropriated the divine "cover-up" of sin.

Knowing God and Abiding in God (2:3-5)

3—The author now asserts his strong moral emphasis. A certainty of our faith arises from the degree to which faith expresses itself in moral living. To precisely what **this** refers is far from clear. The Greek, *en toutō*, may point either back to a previous thought or forward to what is to follow in the sentence. **This** is a common expression in 1 John (cf., e.g., 2:3; 3:10; 5:2). In this case, it seems certain that the antecedent of **this** is found in **keep his commandments. We may be sure that we know him** is, literally, "we know that we have known him" (a present tense followed by a perfect). The verb "to **know**" (*ginōskein*) is found 25 times in 1 John, and is used in two quite distinct senses, as it is in this verse: (1) "be **sure** or certain" (3:19, 24; 4:2, 13; 5:2), and (2) "to be related to God (or Christ)" (11 times, e.g., 2:13; 3:1, 6; 4:6, 7, 8; 5:20). Whether the latter meaning is to be understood in the same sense as is found in the Gospel of John (e.g., 8:9; 14:7) is debatable, but that seems to be the case. To **know** God is to live in a relationship of love and obedience with **him,** not unlike the OT use of "know" (Hebrew, *yadah*, e.g., Hosea 4:6).[13] Our author employs this verb with a certain intentional ambiguity.

The assurance of one's relationship with God stems from the degree to which she or he **keeps his commandments.** At least four times (3:22, 24; 5:3; and here) our author uses the expression **keep.** The parallelism in which it is used with "obey" (5:2, literally, "do"; *poieō*) demonstrates that the two words are synonymously employed (cf. John 14:15). 1 John 3:23 suggests that by **commandments** the author understands the injunctions to believe in Christ and to love other Christians.

4—The negative of v. 3 is now stated, to drive home the point. Claims to a relationship with God accompanied by failure to believe (properly) in Christ and love other Christians demonstrate falsehood. **Disobeys** is actually "not keeping," in parallelism with the previous verse. For **liar** cf. 1:10 and 1:6 above. For **the truth is not in him** cf. 1:8 above and v. 5 below. The same discrepancy between confession and action which is the subject of 1:6-10 is the issue here. The author's point is that a saving relationship with God must, of necessity, reflect itself in a righteous quality of life. But the polemical tone of these words is clear. The separatists, whom the author attacks and against whom he wants to defend the readers, claim to **know** God, yet do not share the author's view of Christ (4:2-3) and do not exercise what he understands to be a loving relationship with the community of Christians (4:20).

5a—The first part of this verse states the positive of what v. 4 has declared in a negative form. Now, however, **word** (*logos*) is used instead of "commandment." There is no distinction between the two (cf. 2:7 below). **Word** is essentially the content of the revelation in Christ (cf. 1:10 above), and for this author that content includes the imperatives of proper belief and love. Another variation from the language of vv. 3-4 is **love for God** instead of "knowing him." For "love," the Johannine Epistles regularly use *agapē*, with *philos* found only once (3 John 15). No sharp distinction between these two words is required, even as the epilog to the Gospel of John shows (21:15-17).

The phrase **love for God** conceals a problematic ambiguity in the Greek which reads, *hē agapē tou theou* ("the love of God"). The Greek can be understood several ways: (1) Human love for God (an objectival genitive, as the RSV understands it); (2) God's love of humanity (a subjectival genitive); (3) human love which has a divine quality (a qualificational genitive). Unfortunately, all three possibilities make some sense in the present verse, and we cannot be sure which the author had in mind, if indeed he intended one to the exclusion of the others. In this document the **love** God has for humanity is inseparably bound to the love humans have as a result, and their love is characterized by its divine source and nature (4:16-21).

In him . . . **perfected** (*en toutō* . . . *teteleiōtai,* literally, "in this one has been **perfected**") means that **love** reaches its highest form in faithfulness to the imperatives of the gospel. The Greek for "perfected" (*teleioō*) may be variously translated, to "fulfill," "accomplish," "complete," or "finish." In Greek thought its sense is the epitome of excellence on a moral continuum; in Hebraic conceptuality its meaning would be closer to "wholeness" or "fullness." Our author means that (1) human **love** for God is mature when it issues in obedience, and/or (2) God's love has its maximum effect on humans when obedience results.

5b—The author returns to the issue of assurance—**we may be sure** (literally, "we know"—and thus to the language used in v. 3 (cf. above). **We are in him** raises one of the common themes in this writing. Our author uses the expression "to be in" some 18 times. Sometimes it describes the relationship of the Christian with God (as here), sometimes with Christ (5:20), and sometimes with the Spirit (4:4). It also describes the relationship of the Christian with the word or love of God (1:10; 2:15), truth (e.g., 1:8), or sin (3:5) (cf. 1:7; 2:10; 4:17, 18). (For the relationship of this usage to the language of the Fourth Gospel, cf. Brown, *Epistles,* pp. 195-196.) For our author the expression describes that relationship which determines one's being. To be *in* something or someone is the primary factor which shapes the character and behavior of the person. There is no mysticism suggested by this phrase; it is, rather, the existential self-understanding which is formative of human personality (cf. Malatesta). For this author obedience to the demand that one believe in the revelation of God in Christ and express love for other believers provides the proof that that person's life is shaped by God.

6—The author now summarizes the argument of vv. 3-5. Confession needs to show itself in life-style. **Abides in** is another of the author's favorite expressions to describe the way in which a human life is determined by a fundamental relationship. In essence, this expression means the same as "to be in" (cf. v. 5b above). The Christian is sometimes said to **abide in** God (e.g., 3:24), in Christ (e.g., 3:6), or both (2:24). God **abides in** the Christian (e.g., 4:12), as does God's word (2:14), the gospel (2:24), and the Christian's anointing (2:27). The author's opponents are described by the absence of the abiding of eternal life and love of God (3:15, 17) in them (cf. 2:10; 3:14; 4:16). (For the relationship of this expression to its appearance in the Gospel of John, cf. Brown, *Epistles*, pp. 259-261.) It is clear that our author's language is shaped by the intimate relationship among the Father, Son, Spirit, and believer found in the theology of the Fourth Gospel.

He says repeats the theme of confession found throughout this section (e.g., 1:10), and **walk** the theme of life-style (e.g., v. 3). For **walk** cf. 1:6 above. **Ought** suggests logical obligation arising from given realities (cf. 3:16; 4:11). The remainder of the verse is, literally translated, "as that one walked also himself so to walk," a clumsy comparison at best. **He** (*ekeinos*, "that one") is ambiguous. The author regularly uses *ekeinos*, however, to refer to Christ (e.g., 3:16; 4:17), although in other cases it can ambiguously refer to Christ or God (e.g., 3:7). Since **walked** means a human life-style, it seems that here "that one" refers to Christ. It is sometimes argued that *ekeinos* became a kind of honorific title for Jesus—"that one around whom we center our lives." Obviously, the author here invokes the life of the human Jesus as a model of obedience and concludes his argument with this sanction.

Verses 3-6 begin with the general assertion that confidence in faith emerges from obedience (v. 3). Then comes an antithetical parallelism which affirms that true Christian faith involves obedience (vv. 4-5a). Finally, the section returns to the general affirmation with which it began (vv. 5b-6). This unit is related to the previous sections in that it declares that the liberation from sin affirmed in 1:8—2:2 can be known as an accomplished fact by means of obedience. Further uniting the three subsections of 1:8—2:6 is the insistence on the logical association of confession and life (compare 1:8 and 2:6).

The Light of the New Commandment (2:7-11)

As 1:5—2:11 began with a reference to light, so now it is brought to a conclusion with that metaphor. The final section deals with the new commandment and with the way in which that imperative sheds light in human life.

The New/Old Commandment (2:7-8)

7—**Beloved** (*agapētos*) occurs six times in 1 John as a form of address. It reflects the author's enactment of his conviction that the community is one in which there is mutual love. **New . . . old commandment** seems confusing at first reading. The **new commandment** is surely the injunction to "love one another" (John 13:34), which the author and his community claim as part of their tradition. It is **old** in the sense that it has been part of their tradition and of the readers' orientation **from the beginning** (cf. 1:1 above). Here **beginning** would seem to mean the initial faith of the readers. Hence, the community should embrace the commandment without question, yet the author's opponents apparently do not do so to his satisfaction. The author can call it **new** in the next verse, because it is new in Christ. He is appealing to the basic orientation the community has received in its tradition. For **word** cf. 1:1 above.

8—That the **new commandment . . . is true in him and in you** means that its reliability for the readers' lives is found in its source. "Truth" is Johannine language for the content of the revelation (cf. 1:8 above), but here **true** has the sense of "correct." The commandment has been proven sound both by God's confirmation of Christ's teachings and in the life experience of the Christian.

Because translates *hoti* ("that"), which may have the sense of (1) how the commandment is proven true, (2) why it is new, or (3) some combination of the two. The meaning is that, because of the eschatological situation of the community, the **commandment** has shown itself to be **true.** Since the old order is giving way to the **new,** the injunction to love one another evokes the quality of life required in this new situation. Life in the kingdom of God requires a new life stance which is harmonious with the new nature of the situation. For **darkness** and **light** cf. 1:5 above. **True light** distinguishes the revelation of Christ from all other claims to revelatory truth. This revelation is **already** an accomplished reality, so that the present situation of the believer is new. The result is that the old situation is still present, to some degree, but is doomed to annihilation—**is passing away.**

Because of the drastic revolution effected by the revelation of God in Christ, the commandment to love one another provides the only appropriate life-style. That commandment is the readers' essential grasp of what it means to live in the new situation brought into being by what God has done.

Light and Love (2:9-11)

The logical consequences of what the author has just established in vv. 7-8 are now explored in a series of three statements. The first (v. 9) and third (v. 11) are essentially synonymous: One who hates is still in darkness. The second (v. 10) affirms that one who loves lives in the embrace of the revelation.

9—The author again stresses that confession without the appropriate behavior is meaningless (cf. 2:4 above). For **light** and **darkness** cf. 1:5 above. To embrace the revelation means to love. **Hate** is symptomatic of having one's orientation for life still within the realm of alienation from God. The contrast of "to love" and "to **hate**" is typically Johannine (cf. John 12:25), and reflects a Semitic tendency toward use of extremes (e.g., Prov. 13:24). There is no such thing as an in-between position (e.g., indifference), but only the two ways. **Hate** occurs four additional times in 1 John (e.g., 3:15) and is the author's characterization of the separatists whose actions do not, in his opinion, reflect an attitude of love toward the community.

Brother refers to other Christians of the community. It is used 14 times in this writing (e.g., 5:16), and is a common NT word for believers (e.g., Col. 1:1). That the term is a masculine expression reflects only the predominance of the patriarchal culture of the first-century world; its meaning embraces those of both sexes. The primary question involved in its appearance in the Johannine epistles has to do with its inclusiveness. Is it a reference to *all* Christians or only to those of the Johannine community? The latter is most probably the case, as Brown has shown (cf. *Epistles*, pp. 269-274). The Johannine tradition apparently knows nothing of the command to love those outside the Christian community (contrast Matt. 5:44, but cf. note 17).

10—The author now states the opposite of his assertion in v. 9. To **love** those of the Christian community is evidence of truly embracing the revelation. **Light** designates the content of the revelation for humans (cf. v. 8 above), and to **abide** in that **light** means to have one's fundamental life orientation determined by the revelation. For **abide** cf. v. 6 above. **In it there is no cause for stumbling** is literally, "offense in him [or 'it'] is not." It (Greek, *autō*) may as well be rendered "him" and hence is ambiguous as to whether it refers to **light** or to the one who **loves. Cause for stumbling** loosely translates *skandalon*. The word has the basic meaning of "a trap," but is used in the NT for that which offends another (e.g., John 6:61) or tempts one to unfaithfulness (e.g., Rev. 2:14). Alternative interpretations of the clause in this verse are: (1) The believer who loves finds nothing in the revelation which is offensive, and hence there is no internal conflict. (2) The believer who loves does not offend others within the community. In the first case, *autō* is taken as "it" and, in the second case, as **him.** *Skandalon* in either case has a double sense of being offensive and endangering faithfulness. Given the situation of the author, the second interpretation seems the more likely. In the loving Christian there is nothing which threatens the integrity of the community, as opposed to those who refuse to practice love and thereby cause division and apostasy among members of the church.

11—The author returns to the description of those who fail to behave in a loving fashion, and essentially repeats the point of v. 9 (cf. above). For **walks** cf. 1:6, above. The author expands the metaphorical sense of **walks** with **does not know where he is going.** Without love, which means without benefit of the revelation, one's journey in life is without direction, purpose, or meaning. It is like trying to make a journey in the pitch blackness of night (cf. John 11:9-10). Blindness is the condition of one bereft of the revelation of God and its consequent loving life-style. **Blinded** in Johannine vocabulary, is, in effect, unbelief (e.g., John 9:40-41). The tautological character of the verse (three occurrences of the word **darkness,** and the repetition of the same point in the last two clauses [**does not know** through **blinded his eyes**]) has the character of an oral reinforcement of the theme. **Know** (in this case, *oida*) is a word related to perception. But its meaning is the same as **know** in 2:3 (cf. above).

In 1:5—2:11 our author has explored the meaning of God's act in Christ for the readers' immediate situation. He has claimed that the divine act provides fellowship, cleansing, forgiveness, and love among those who correctly understand it. To embrace the revelation has certain inescapable implications for the way one lives, the most important of which are a continual reliance on God for forgiveness of sin and a loving posture toward other believers. Our skillful author has wrapped all of this in the package of a light/darkness metaphor, poetically tying together his diverse themes. The thrust is toward the assurance and commendation of the readers' basic stance over against those who have threatened that stance with their own beliefs and practices. As a description of the life of the Christian this passage captures the most essential characteristics.

■ The Believers and the World (2:12-17)

This problematic little section has been linked to the previous unit by the association of the words "sin" in 2:12 and "walks in darkness" in 2:11. Beyond this tie there is little that shows a logical progression.

This section is concerned with the victory of believers—what has been accomplished for them by the gospel. It is comprised of three parts: (1) A dramatic declaration of the accomplishment of the gospel for the community (vv. 12-14); (2) an exhortation to live free of the world, along with a description of the destiny and nature of the world (vv. 15-16); and (3) a contrast of the world and the believer (v. 17). The three are in the indicative, the imperative, and the indicative, in that order. The author has skillfully interwoven what realities have been established by God and what demands upon humans emerge from those realities.

The Victory of Believers (2:12-14)

These three verses constitute what is one of the most debated passages of 1 John. It is necessary to consider it as a whole before attending to individual verses. The subunit is a pair of triplets (*A, B, C, a, b, c*) with two stylistic variations signaling the transition from the first to the second—the switch from "little children" (*teknia*) in v. 12 to "children" (*paidia*) in v. 13c, and the shift from "am writing" (*graphō*) used in vv. 12, 13a, and 13b to "write" (*egrapsa*) in vv. 13c, 14a, and 14b.

The variation of addressees is still another feature of this passage: v. 12, "little children" (*teknia*); vv. 13a and 14a, "fathers" (*pateres*); vv. 13b and 14b, "young men" (*neaniskoi*); and v. 13c, "children" (*paidia*). With the exception of the variation between *teknia* and *paidia* the six are a perfect pair of three. The question as to whom these words designate is often raised and involves at least two subordinate questions. The first is how many groups are addressed through these six words. Should we imagine four groups, with "little children" and "children" constituting different groups; three groups, with the two aforementioned words designating a single group; or one group, for which each word is appropriate in a different way? The second concern is with the issue of whether or not these words (or any one of them) are used in the sense of official leaders and hence are in some sense titles.

It seems most unlikely that any of these addressees are formal leaders. In spite of arguments to the contrary (cf. e.g., Houlden, pp. 70-71) there is no solid evidence that would support such a conjecture. A simpler explanation is that the words are used to refer to Christians of different levels of maturity within the same community. Hence, we are to think of "fathers" as those who have been Christians for the longest period of time and who have achieved a greater maturity in the faith than the others. "Children" and "little children" would be two labels for one group— those whose faith is the newest and whose maturation as Christians has only begun. Somewhere in between are the "young men," whose level of experience in the new faith exceeds that of the "children" but is not yet equal to the "fathers." It appears more likely that the terms are used metaphorically for "spiritual" rather than actual chronological age (compare 1 Cor. 3:1-3).

One difficulty with this view is that "little children" and "children" seem to be used elsewhere in the document as forms of address for all Christians (e.g., 2:1,18). This confusing fact can be explained as a simple variation of style on the part of the author. In the list we have before us, he uses "children" and "little children" in comparison with other Christians; in cases such as 2:1 and 18 he uses the terms in reference to the relationship of all Christians to God. That such a variation should occur is made more plausible by the suggestion that the individual units of 1 John were written at different times and then brought together into one document without extensive editing (cf. Introduction §2).

Another problem posed in this passage is the shift from "am writing" (*graphō*, present tense, vv. 12, 13a, and 13b) to "write" (*egrapsa*, aorist tense, vv. 13c, 14a, and 14b). Some have proposed that the latter verb refers to a previous document written to the readers, while the former is used of this one. It seems more likely that the two represent a simple variation in style, in this case to mark the transition from the first to the second pair of triplets. This author varies the tense of this verb rather freely, as is evidenced in 1:4; 2:1,7,8 (where the present is used) and 2:21,26; 5:13 (where the aorist is employed). Such style variation is the easiest explanation of the difference between "little children" (v. 12) and "children" (v. 13c) as well.

Finally, the meaning of the word *because* must be considered. Each of the six sentences includes a form of the verb *to write*, the term *to you*, an addressee, and a clause beginning with the connective *because*. The precise sense of the connective is not clear. The basic alternatives are twofold: (1) a causal relationship ("I am writing to you since [or 'because'] this or that"—so the RSV and most modern translations), or (2) a declarative relationship ("I am writing to you [to say] this or that"—cf. Haas, de Jonge, and Swellengrebel, p. 55). It may be that the two senses should not be sharply distinguished (cf. Marshall, pp. 136-137), but the declarative connection seems more logical. Why the content of the *because* clauses should motivate the author's writing is not at all clear. On the other hand, taking the clauses as declarations of the state of the addressees' lives renders the passage meaningful.

12—For **little children** cf. the previous paragraphs. For **sins are forgiven** cf. 1:9 above. **For his sake** is literally, "on account of his name." The expression reflects our author's basic understanding of the cross as an act by which Christ sacrificially atoned for **sins** (cf. 2:2 above). He uses *name* two additional times (3:23 and 5:13), and in each case it has the meaning of "identity" as it often does in the Hebraic-Jewish tradition.

13a—**Fathers** (*pateres*) refers to the "pillars" of the community, whose experience in the faith has brought them maturity and wisdom. This is the only time the author uses this word to refer to humans (contrast, e.g., 2:13). Their maturity lies in the fact that they have an intimate relationship with God (**know him,** cf. 2:3 above). For **from the beginning** cf. 2:7, above. Here it means the beginning of faith.

13b—**Young men** (*neaniskoi*) occurs only here and in v. 14. Those in the middle range of Christian maturation are assured that they have **overcome the evil one.** The verb **overcome** (*nikaō*) has the sense of "to conquer or prevail in combat" (cf. 4:4; 5:4,5). **Evil one** translates *ponēros*, a personification of evil used again in 5:18, 19 and found as one of the fourth evangelist's words for the opposition to God (John 17:15). Our author uses "devil" (e.g., 3:10), "spirit of error" (4:6), "the antichrist" (e.g., 4:3), and "the evil one" interchangeably. The result of the gospel is that evil is for all effects defeated.

13c—Our author uses this Greek word for **children** (*paidia*) only one other time (2:18), and there in the sense of Christians in general. **You know the Father** is a variation of the clause found in 13a used of the "fathers." This shows that the least mature of the Christians, too, share a relationship with God. For **know** cf. 2:3 above. For **Father** cf. 1:2 above.

14a—This verse repeats exactly 13a (cf. above). It shows the author's lack of skill in the construction of his otherwise rather artistic passage, but it also demonstrates his predilection for repetition.

14b—Three statements are found in the **because** clause in this case: (1) **strong** (the only use of this word in 1 John) means powerful in a spiritual sense (e.g., 1 Cor. 4:10). (2) **Word of God** is a variation of "word of life" (cf. 1:1 above). For **abides in you** cf. 2:6 above. (3) For **overcome** . . . cf. 13b above. The latter is another exact repetition.

The victory of the believers described in the *because* clauses of the passage is impressive. Sins are forgiven (v. 12); a relationship with God is established (vv. 13a, c, 14a); evil is defeated (13b, 14b); spiritual strength is given (14b); and the center of life is the gospel message (14b). No exact correlation between the levels of maturity and specific gifts should be read into the passage. The list of benefits is intended to be general—to describe the range of gifts bestowed upon those embraced by the revelation. Taken together they constitute a summary of the victory of the believers in Christ.

The Nature and Destiny of the World (2:15-16)

In these verses the author exhorts those who have experienced the victory in Christian faith to free themselves of the influence of the realm of unbelief. If vv. 12-14 declare what God has ac-

complished in the lives of the believers, vv. 15-16 emphasize what
the believer must accomplish.

The Believer and the Love of the World (2:15-16)

15—**Love** is used here in the sense of a contrast between extremes, as the author employs the radical contrast of love and
hate in 2:10-11. For **love** cf. 2:10. **World** (Greek, *kosmos*) is another of the features of Johannine dualism the author employs
(cf. "light and darkness," 2:9 above). **World** is used often in the
Gospel of John for the realm of unbelief and alienation from God
(e.g., 17:14). It is in this symbolic sense that our author uses the
term most often in his writing (e.g., 4:5; 5:4), and so it is here.
Like the fourth evangelist, however, the author of 1 John can use
the term in a descriptive, nondualistic way as well (e.g., 2:2).
Things in the world should be understood, therefore, not in the
sense of material objects but as those realities which are rooted
and have their existence in that which is foreign to God. (Compare
the use of "being in," 2:5 above.) This is in contrast to **love for
the Father is not in him.** The **love** that is **in** one determines that
person's basic orientation, and with typical Johannine exclusivistic
dualism there can be only one or the other fundamental loyalty—
to the world or to God. The "if . . . then . . ." construction is
one of the author's favorite ways to stress inescapable consequences (cf. 1:6-10 above).

16—The author now attempts to describe the nature of that
which constitutes the realm of opposition to God. For **in the world**
see v. 15 above. **All** includes everything which owes its existence
to that which is alien to God. The author now itemizes three
features of the realm of unbelief. **Lust** (*epithymia*) is "desire" or
"longing" which may have as its object something evil or something good. The RSV **lust** unfortunately may tend to suggest to
the modern reader only a sexual connotation, which is narrower
than the meaning our author intends. **Flesh** (*sarx*) denotes human
life in and of itself, not necessarily evil or materialistic. The desires of humans, apart from what God wants for them, are rooted

in a separation from the Creator of life. The desires of the **eyes** are the longings to possess that which can be seen as opposed to that which is unseen and eternal.

The pride of life is a difficult phrase, for it may mean "the life of which persons are proud" or "the pride which arises from life." **Pride** designates a boastful attitude which finds fulfillment in what persons claim they accomplish for themselves. **Life** translates *bios*, which is used for physical, biological existence. The phrase taken as a whole, then, would mean any attitude which lays claim to being independently responsible for existence, without acknowledgment of a Creator.

These three items ("lust of the flesh," "lust of the eyes," and "pride of life") have in common an orientation which sees life as an attainment to be desired in and for itself without reference to an ultimate dependence upon God. Such an orientation is **of the world** (literally, "out of the world"), meaning "founded on that which is alien to God and not rooted in the ultimate." The expression **is of** is one of the ways by which the fourth evangelist speaks of that orientation which determines a person's character and destiny (e.g., John 10:32).

In these two verses the author has attempted to persuade the readers that the victory given them in Christ requires that their lives evince a posture of dependence on God and an orientation away from all illusions of existence without such a dependence.

The Passing World and the Abiding Believer (2:17)

17—A closing affirmation moves from the imperative of vv. 15-16 back to the indicatives of vv. 12-14. The question addressed here is what is finally important in life—what is ultimate. That which is not aligned with God (**the world**) is in truth only penultimate, while harmony with the ultimate reality is lasting. **Passes away** means that the process of annihilation is underway and implies the imminent end of that which is opposed to God. That the author believed in the imminence of the end is evident in v. 18. For **lust** cf. v. 16 above. In contrast to the annihilation

of all that is alienated from God is **he who does the will of God.**
Relationship with God for our author is defined by behavior
("doing"). For **abides** cf. 2:6 above. **For ever** in the Greek is
literally "into the age." In the Gospel of John the expression is
used of partaking of Christian existence (e.g., 4:14 and 6:51), but
here it is intended in contrast with **passes away** and suggests
duration. In faithfulness to **God** one finds that which is ultimate
and of lasting value.

The section frames the exhortation for the Christian to live free
of the misorientation of that which is separated from God (vv. 15-
16) with declarations of what is given to humanity in the gospel
(vv. 12-14) and the enduring consequences of the gospel (v. 17).

■ Truth and Lie (2:18-29)

What unifies these verses is the eschatological framework within which the author discusses the crisis and uncertainty brought
about by the action of the separatists. The section begins with
reference to the "last hour" (v. 18) and concludes with allusions
to the parousia (v. 28). It is positioned here by our author because
of the fact that the preceding section has ended with a reference
to the approaching demise of evil. Hence, the expressions "the
world passes away" (v. 17a) and "last hour" (v. 18) are the threads
which sew the sections together, however loosely.

The section is comprised of three parts: (1) A discussion of the
antichrists, and what constitutes opposition to Christ—an eschatological interpretation of the community crisis (vv. 18-23); (2)
an assuring word that the believer is protected from the falsehood
of the antichrists, i.e., the separatists (vv. 24-27); and (3) an exhortation to faithfulness made powerful by reference to the parousia (vv. 28-29). The section informs us how seriously our author
views the schism, and demonstrates the manner in which the
readers are encouraged not to lose their confidence as a result of
the crisis. The author's pastoral persuasiveness—the arguments
he invokes to convince the readers—is most instructive.

The Antichrists (2:18-23)

The thought of these verses moves from the announcement of the "last hour" and the appearance of the antichrists (v. 18) to the condemnation of the separatists (v. 19), to the distinction between them and the true believers (vv. 20-21), and finally to a definition of the antichrists (vv. 22-23). The subunit is thus enclosed within references to the antichrists and clearly issues the judgment that those who have separated themselves from the community are the infamous antichrists of the end-time.

18—Children (*paidia*) here means all Christians (cf. vv. 12 and 13 above). **Last hour** means the final period before the concluding act of God in the history of the world and humanity. It is used in this document only here and in v. 18. The more common NT designation is "last day(s)" (e.g., John 6:40,44,54; 11:24; 12:48; 2 Tim. 3:1; Heb. 1:2; James 5:3; 2 Peter 3:3). The use of **hour** rather than "day(s)" is a peculiar variation which may be an intentional effort to declare the nearness of the decisive time. It may also be that the Johannine tradition in which Jesus' glorification in the cross is spoken of as "hour" (e.g., John 2:4; 7:30; 8:20) has influenced our author.

Associated with the eschaton in apocalyptic imagery is the figure which represents the culmination of all that is opposed to God and efforts to perfect creation (cf. especially Revelation 12). However, the term **antichrist** (*antichristos*) is found only in 1 and 2 John (cf. 2:22; 4:3; and 2 John 7) and has no precedent in OT, intertestamental, NT, or Rabbinic literature.[14] Brown shows, however, how disparate motifs have been wedded to coin this expression (*Epistles,* pp. 333-336). The author or the Johannine community has epitomized the opposing force and its insurgence at the final period of salvation history with the concept of a figure who stands in direct contradiction to Christ.

The author's argument is that: the appearance of such a figure has been expected (**you have heard**), many such figures have now appeared, and **therefore** the end is upon us. Such an expectation of the advent of opponents of Christ is not rooted in the Gospel of John, although other roots in early Christian tradition are discernible (e.g., Mark 13:5). The plural, **antichrists,** shows that the tradition upon which the author builds is not fixed. But the logic of the argument implies that the community embraced some sort of apocalyptic image of the **last** days. This verse has greatest affinities with Mark 13 and Revelation, and few with the Gospel of John.

19—This verse turns attention to those who have apparently separated themselves from the community (cf. Introduction §3). It says of them that (1) it is they who separated themselves from the community and (2) by doing so they demonstrated that they were never really part of the community. **They went out from us** seems to mean that the group had not been expelled but left by their own volition. The first clause plays upon the Greek preposition *ek* ("from" or "of"). The verb **went out** is aorist, meaning a completed action of the past; the verb **were,** on the other hand, is imperfect, suggesting an enduring situation from the past. The separatists were never **of us** in the sense that they had never truly embraced the gospel, as our author understands it. His argument is circular, for he defines being "of us" as continuing with the community; since they have not done so, they are not "of us." The preposition **of** in the expression "of us" is used in the sense of having one's basic orientation and commitment (cf. John 8:44). **Continued** is a translation of a form of the verb "to abide" (cf. 2:6 above), and suggests a close, enduring relationship. **It might be plain** means that their behavior revealed their true identity—**not** one **of us.** It is clear that the author is attempting to explain the schism in the community on two grounds: (1) It is part of the events of the eschaton (v. 18), and (2) it is a result of the fact that the separatists never shared a genuine faith with the community.

20—The subject now moves slightly to clarify the distinction between the author's community and the separatists—a distinction stated in the previous verse. This is done by making claims for the nature of the author's community, which by implication is in contradistinction to the separatists. The community has been anointed and hence they **know. Anointed** (*chrisma*) is problematic. The term is found only in this epistle (here and 2:27). The crucial questions are: (1) Is this a reference to a physical act of anointing or is it a metaphorical allusion? (2) If the former, does it speak of Baptism or an anointing practiced by the Johannine community? (3) And, if the latter, with what is the metaphor compared—e.g., the gift of the Spirit or the reception of the gospel (cf. Brown, *Epistles*, pp. 342-348)? Interpreters are divided on the resolution of these questions, and no final answer can be given. However, given the context of the epistle it seems more likely that the anointing is a metaphor for the gift of the Spirit. In 5:6 the Spirit is called a "witness," and here anointing is connected with knowing. It is conceivable that the Johannine community valued a tradition of the role of the Spirit which brought assurance to the believers (cf., e.g., John 16:13). This *chrisma* may have been associated with Baptism, but the evidence leaves the determination of that question beyond reach. Equally possible is that some practice of anointing with oil was associated with the initiation of believers into the community.[15]

The Holy One (*tou hagiou*) is the source of the anointing. This is the only use of **holy** by our author, so it is not clear if it refers here to God, Christ, or the Spirit. **Holy** is a common OT adjective for God (e.g., Hos. 11:9), but in the NT God is never called "the Holy One." Numerous passages, however, speak of Jesus as "the Holy One" (of God) (e.g., Rev. 3:7; Mark 1:24). While the Spirit is never designated with this title, the adjective **holy** is commonly used of the Spirit (e.g., Acts 10:45; John 14:26). The majority of scholars take the reference here to be to Christ. Still, if the anointing is a metaphorical expression for the gift of the Spirit, might it not be the case that the source of the anointing is now designated metaphorically with the title **the Holy One**?

The result of the gift of the Spirit is knowledge. Textual variants make uncertain whether the **all** is the object of the verb (*panta*—"all things") or whether it goes with the subject (*pantes*—**you all**). The former is more easily explained as a scribal correction than the latter, making **you all** the better reading. Then, however, what the scribes were trying to correct becomes our problem. What is it that the author believes his readers **know** (*oidate*)? The answer is found in the next verse where the readers are assured that they know the truth.

21—For **I write to you** cf. 2:14 above. For **truth** and **lie** cf. 1:6 above. **Know** (*oidate*) has the sense of intellectual comprehension but also personal participation (cf. John 8:32). The author assures the community that it is correct in its position and not guilty of the errors of the separatists.

22—Now comes the theological definition of *lie* and the first clear indication of the Christological difference between the separatists and the author's community. **The liar** is one who stands opposed to the truth of the faith. The title (here used with the definite article, **the**) may have been a formal designation for an apocalyptic figure identified with or closely associated with the antichrists in late Johannine thought, but the other uses of the word in the document do not provide clear evidence to that effect (1:10; 2:4; 4:20; 5:10). For the author the opposition is a false doctrine, namely, a faulty view of **Christ.** It is the denial of the identity of the historical figure, **Jesus,** with the Christ. While it is not clear precisely *how* the separatists denied **that Jesus is the Christ,** 4:2 would suggest that it is the historical, human nature of Jesus that is the issue. The author attacks a view of Christ which apparently does not, to his satisfaction, acknowledge the full historicity of the Christ. That the separatists fully denied the humanity of God's revealer is not clear, but their view seems to have bordered on such docetism. The gnostic Christians whose library has been discovered at Nag Hammadi (Egypt) apparently stressed that Christ took many and various forms and not only the form of the man Jesus. It may be that the view of the separatists was a forerunner of that later form of gnostic Christology.

The author and his opponents represent two different interpretations of the Johannine tradition. The first takes seriously the assertions of the humanity of Jesus in the Fourth Gospel (e.g., 1:14) and has been influenced by the general Christian tradition which fully identified the historical man, Jesus, with the Christ, while the second emphasizes the divine character of the Johannine Jesus (e.g., John 1:1) and has perhaps been influenced by the tendency toward docetism (or a polymorphism) in late first-century Christianity. The author charges that those who oppose his view are none other than **the antichrist** (cf. v. 18 above). The charge is furthered by the claim that a denial of the historicity of God's revelation in Jesus is a denial of God himself. For **Father** and **Son** cf. 1:2-3 above. The reader could possibly infer from this sentence the separatists' theological, as well as a Christological, difference from the author. However, to argue from this evidence that the separatists were atheistic, or that they held to a gnostic distinction between a creator and a father God, is to press the verse too hard. Rather, it appears the author means to say that a "faulty" Christology produces a misguided view of God.

23—This verse makes the point clear. To reject the humanity of Christ has the result of depriving one of a relationship with the God revealed in the human Messiah. The use of **Father/Son** here and in v. 22b has the effect of stressing the close relationship of the revealer and the God thereby revealed. **Has the father** means to be related to God, to be a child of God.

Verses 22-23 betray the fact that our author assumes that there is a "correct" doctrine, an orthodoxy, which is essential for a salvific relationship with God. Failure to embrace that "right" doctrine, deviation from the perimeters of that single view, deprives one of the benefits of the revelation. The attachment of such significance to the conceptions one holds of Christ is a monumental development in the church. The emergence of the norm for correct doctrine is one of the characteristics of late NT literature (e.g., 2 Tim. 4:3; 1 Tim. 3:9; 6:2b-3; 2 John 9). To be sure, such attention to correct belief is anticipated in both Paul (e.g., Gal. 1:19) and John (e.g., 14:10-11), but for our author the precise content of correct belief has now been determined, at least with regard to the person of Christ. Denial of that doctrine is characteristic of the eschatological opposition to God. The first epistle of John condemns such misconceptions in the strongest possible words, while also trying too to assure the faithful of the correctness of their view.

Protection from the Lie (2:24-27)

Having depicted the seriousness of the situation brought about by the separatists and their views, the author attempts to affirm his community in its stance. They are protected from the evil power of the "lie" which is propagated by the opponents and which expresses the last efforts of those forces alien to God to thwart the divine plan of salvation. Their protection resides in the enduring results of the gospel (vv. 24-25) and in their anointing (vv. 26-27). The pastoral quality of the author is evident here as exhortation is mingled with affirmation.

24—The section begins with an imperative. **What you heard** refers to the proclamation of the gospel message (cf. 1:3). For **from the beginning** cf. 1:1; 2:7,13,14, above. For **abide** cf. 2:6 above. The readers are urged to maintain a close relationship with the gospel message which brought them to faith and to cling to that message amid the crisis facing the church. The second sentence of the verse claims that such concentration on the gospel assures a continuing relationship with God and Christ. For **abides in** cf. 2:14 above. For **Father/Son** cf. 1:2 and 7 above. The author calls the believers back to their roots in faith—to their origin as Christians—where there is security in time of danger.

25—The results of the gospel message are a relationship with God and **eternal life** (cf. 1:2 above). The emphasis of the Greek is upon the **promise**—literally, "the promise he promised." This is the only use of "promise" (Greek, *epangelia*) in 1 John. In threatening times the readers are reminded of God's promise of their new life with God. **This** may refer to either the "abiding" of v. 24 or **eternal life. He** is ambiguous, insofar as its antecedent may be either God or Christ.

26—This verse makes clear the urgency of the imperative and the assurance of vv. 24-25. There are those—the separatists— who would **deceive** the readers. The Greek word for **deceive** occurs three times in 1 John—here, 1:8 (cf. above), and 3:7. Its use in 3:7 is similar to its meaning here. There are those who would lead the reader into 'an erroneous view (cf. 4:6 below). Deception is sometimes understood to be one of the characteristic tools of the efforts of evil at the last day (e.g., Rev. 12:9), and therefore it is likely that the deceivers are closely aligned in our author's mind with the antichrists (cf. 2:18 above). The threat of deception is real and present, our author believes, and the readers must be on guard against it. Again, it appears the situation brought about by the separatists is viewed in eschatological proportions.

27a—As it is in v. 20 (cf. above), **the anointing** (*to chrisma*) protects the reader from the threat of the deceivers. The presence and power of the Spirit at work in the believers is what enables them to hold to the truth of the gospel and withstand all the challenges to their confidence. The anointing is, again as it appears in 2:20, a fact of the past—**which you received. From him** is likewise as ambiguous in its designation of the source of the anointing as "the Holy One" in 2:20. But, if our interpretation of 2:20 is correct, the author is referring to a bestowal of divine presence by the Spirit, and now claims that that presence intimately relates to the reader—**abides in you** (cf. 2:14 above). The result of the gift of the divine presence is that the reader has no need to be taught—a remarkable exaggeration. **The anointing** is a teaching which supplies all that the readers ever need. If such were the case, one wonders why the author feels constrained to share his teachings with the community. Obviously, the desire to assure the readers of the correctness of their position over against that of the separatists has moved our author to overstate the case. Apparently, the gift of the Spirit is conceived as bestowing a set of doctrines or views, which shows that the author thinks of the anointing not as an emotional (nor enthusiastic) experience but as a cognitive one (cf. John 2:25 and 16:30).

27b—The Greek of the last half of the verse is comprised of no less than five clauses strung together in a way that produces considerable ambiguity and numerous scribal efforts at reducing that ambiguity. The RSV is probably correct in rendering them as the second half of a compound sentence, but clarity might be increased if the words **and is true** up to **abide in him** were placed in parentheses. So, the sense of the Greek is "remain with the one who has taught you all you need to know, since that one has taught you what is true and not what is false." But the pronouns of the five clauses cloud their meaning. **His** refers, we believe, to the Spirit (cf. v. 20, above), but **it** may also be read "he" (from the Greek verb, *edidaxen*). Is it the **anointing,** or the Spirit who gives it, that is the subject of the verb? Maintaining the personal pronoun seems to make more sense (hence, read "he" instead of **it was taught you**). Finally, the Greek may in the last clause mean **abide in him** (i.e., the Spirit) or "in it" (i.e., the anointing). Either meaning is possible and changes the point very little, but the RSV has better clarity.

If the Greek is obscure, so too is the sense of language. That the Christians have been **taught . . . everything** can only mean that the believers have received in correct form the essentials for faith. The Johannine community held that the Spirit-Paraclete communicates all that the believers yearn to know (John 14:26) and leads them to "all truth," that is, to a full understanding of the revelation of God in Christ (John 16:13). The author of 1 John invokes that belief now as a way of assuring the readers that the "new" teachings of the separatists should not disturb them. They have been **taught** by the Spirit, and that is all on which they need rely; for that is **true,** as opposed to the **lie** offered them by the dissenters (cf. 1:6; 2:21, above; and 4:1, below). **Abide in him** may be translated as an imperative ("you should abide") or as an indicative ("you do abide"). While the decision is difficult, the latter seems more in keeping with the comforting tone of this verse.

The author thus gives the readers reason to trust their present stand and reject the effort of the separatists to sway them. They have in their initial beginnings in the gospel and in the gift of the Spirit the true understanding of the faith, and they are exhorted to remain faithful to that view. They are protected from the falsehood of the separatists by their experiences in the community. It is important that the author ask the readers in a time of uncertainty, when their confidence is challenged, to return to their "roots" in faith—their "beginning" and their "anointing." As Israel gained its confidence in times of trial by remembering its past history, the church is urged to tap the source of its stability—what God has done for it in the past.

Confidence for the End (2:28-29)

Confidence is the theme of the final verses of chap. 2, as it is of vv. 26-27. This small section is a concluding exhortation to the discussion of the truth of the gospel in distinction from the falsehood of the troublers of the community. The final words appeal to the eschatological day. One can face that day with confidence by "abiding in Christ" (v. 28) and the evidence that one does abide in him is found in examining the quality of one's moral life (v. 29).

These two verses betray a carefully conceived, almost poetic structure which may be displayed in this way:

Little children:
  Abide in him,
    so that
      at his *appearance* we may have confidence, and
      at his *coming* we may not shrink in shame.
    If
      we know that he is *righteous*
      we know that those who do *righteousness* are
  born of him.

The address and the conclusion both suggest divine parentage. The exhortation "abide in him" is paralleled by its result, "born of him." Each verse parallels two thoughts—"appearance" and "coming" in v. 28, and God's righteousness and human righteousness in v. 29. The second verse employs two different Greek words for "know" (*oida* and *ginōskein*) to introduce both parts of the sentence (the protasis and the apodosis).

28—**And now** signals a summary-conclusion, while pointing to the importance of this moment in the community's history (cf. 2:18, "so now"). For **little children** cf. v. 12 above. For **abide** cf. v. 2 above. **In him** in this case means Christ, since **he appears** is an allusion to the parousia. **Appears** translates *phanerōthē*, a verb used eight times in this document. It is used twice of the revelation of the true identity of humans (2:19 and 3:2), four times of God's act in Christ (1:2; 3:5, 8, 9), and twice of Christ's appearance in glory (here and 3:2). Compare 1 Peter 1:20 and 5:4 for similar uses. Confrontation with Christ in the parousia is not an uncommon context for exhortation in the NT (e.g., Matt. 10:32-33; Mark 8:38; Luke 9:26; 2 Tim. 2:12). **We may have** identifies the author with those addressed. **Confidence** translates *parrēsia*, a word which roots in the idea of "speaking openly," "boldly," or "plainly" (e.g., John 16:29). Here it conveys the idea of speaking freely and without guilt with the glorified Christ. Brown says that for the believers Christ "comes as a loving friend, and not as a judge" (*Epistles*, p. 381). Cf. 3:21 below.

Such a confident encounter with Christ is contrasted (in antithetical parallelism) with **not shrink from him in shame** (or "be ashamed"). This is the only Johannine use of the Greek verb *aischynō* (cf. Luke 16:3; 2 Cor. 10:8; Phil. 1:20; 1 Peter 4:16). **At his coming** is literally "in his parousia" (*en tē parousia autou*). The play on the words *parrēsian* (**confidence**) and *parousia* (**coming**) may be intentional. *Parousia* parallels "appearance," and refers to that expected reappearance of Christ in power to complete God's redemptive work. This is the sole use of *parousia* in Johannine literature, even though it is found some 23 times in other NT passages (e.g., Matt. 24:3, 27, 37, 39; 1 Thess. 2:19; James 5:7). The word literally means "presence," and was used for the visit of a king or the manifestation of a hidden deity. In Christian circles it was adapted, along with Jewish concepts of the appearance of the Messiah, to the expectation of God's further work in Christ at the last day. Its use and the complex of ideas associated with

it are another illustration of the prominence of a futuristic eschatology in the late Johannine community, in contrast to the
views of the Fourth Gospel (cf. 2:23 above).

The thought of the verse as a whole is that to maintain one's
relationship with Christ now is to assure a confident reunion with
him at the end-time.

29—There is a shift of argument in this verse, apparently in
order to encourage a faithful moral life and, by implication, to
condemn the separatists whose lives are not, in the author's view,
of acceptable quality (cf. 2:4, 9-11 above). The argument follows
this pattern: If God (or Christ) is **righteous** and if believers live
righteously, believers are of divine parentage. The condition (**if
you know**) is rhetorical. The author is appealing to the basic affirmation—of course, God (or Christ) is **righteous**—in order to
make the logic of the exhortation undeniable. The antecedent of
he is ambiguous and troublesome. "His" in the previous verse is
clearly Christ, but here the reference would seem more logically
to be God. God in 1:9 has been called **righteous,** and the adjective
is attributed to Christ in 2:1. Scholars are divided. The phrase
born of him lends some evidence for thinking it is God who is
meant here, since "born of God" is used in 3:9; 4:7; 5:1, 4, and
18. "Born of Christ" never occurs in 1 John. Between verses 28
and 29 the author has shifted the antecedent in a disconcerting
manner, but the difference between God and Christ seems insignificant at this point. For **righteous** (*dikaios*) cf 1:9 ("just")
above.

On the basis of the truism that God is **righteous,** the author
derives the point. On the use of the Greek *ginōskein* (**be sure**)
to mean "certainty" cf. 2:3 above. The phrase is, literally, "You
know as well that every one doing righteousness (or justice)." The
expression **who does right** has a Semitic quality—living out a
righteousness—and is used three times in 1 John (3:7 and 10, as
well as here; cf. below). It is significant that the only occurrences
of *righteousness* (*dikaiosynē*) in 1 John are in the phrase "who
does right" (2:29; 3:7, 10). *Righteousness* for our author has no

content except as it is expressed in human action (contrast Paul, e.g., Rom. 1:17).

Born of him means that one is rooted in and related to God as a child is to a parent. The phrase is used nine times in six passages in the epistle (here; 3:9 [twice]; 4:7; 5:1 [twice], 4, 18 [twice]). In these passages our author makes a number of statements in describing those who are **born of** God: (1) They live righteously and do not sin (2:29; 3:9; 4:7; 5:18). (2) They believe Jesus is the Christ (5:1). (3) They are victorious over and guarded against evil (5:5, 18).

Behind the thought of our author lies the conceptuality of the Fourth Gospel, which understands that those who are embraced by the revelation have their origin in the divine realm (John 1:13; 3:3-8; 8:39-44). In the theology of the fourth evangelist such a view fits within a dualistic structure which dictated that one be affiliated with either the divine or the evil realm. What distinguishes the view of the author of 1 John is the insistence that it is the *moral* quality of one's life which determines one's parentage, while for the fourth evangelist it is far more a matter of one's response to the revelation (and hence one's view of Jesus) which is the fundamental matter. In a sense, our author's view is profoundly Hebraic, since in the OT obedience constitutes parentage in God (cf. Brown, *Epistles*, p. 385). "Spiritual rebirth" is not really the issue in this document (against Smalley, pp. 134-136), but rather the matter of what it means to be a member of the family of God brought into existence by the revelation in Christ. The moral crisis of the community, aroused by the stance of the separatists, pushed our author to define that family in terms of morality in a way significantly different from the tradition known to the church in the Fourth Gospel.

Two certainties have provided the foundation of the appeal of vv. 28-29: the parousia and the righteousness of God. In the light of those certainties, two appeals are made: that the readers devote themselves above all to their relationship with God/Christ and that they express that relationship in righteous living.

The section 2:18-29 demonstrates that the Johannine church

had adopted a future hope quite different from that which we witness in the Fourth Gospel. It is interesting that the fourth evangelist addressed his community in its time of crisis by pointing to the way in which God's promises for the future were already (but not exclusively) present. The author of 1 John, on the other hand, stresses the future bestowal of those promises. Furthermore, he does so with ample use of a set of images for how God will accomplish the perfection of creation—a set of images usually termed "apocalyptic." Examples of those images in this section are the figure of the antichrist and the "coming" of Jesus.

One might suppose that the church for which 1 John was written had come under the influence of other Christian churches which embraced hopes for the future understood in such "apocalyptic" imagery. The church of the author of 1 John seems to have abandoned in part the emphasis on the realized and present reality of those promises that were part of their tradition. What is evident is that different situations for the church evoke different expressions of the good news message. For our author the situation of the community called for a more vivid portrayal of the divine plan for the future.

■ Children of God and Children of the Devil (3:1-24)

Chapter 3 is devoted to the theme of the children of God, and is connected with the preceding section by the expressions "children of God" (3:1) and "born of him" (2:24). The relevance of this theme for the situation of the community becomes explicit in vv. 4-18 in the contrast of the children of God and children of the devil, but it is implicit throughout the chapter. The author attempts to define and characterize what it means to be of divine parentage in such a way as to fortify the readers over against the separatists. Here we see most clearly a feature of the entire document, namely, its effort to crystallize the *identity* of the Christian community. The position and actions of the separatists in their claim to possess the authentic understanding of Christian life and faith must have caused serious self-doubts among all of the members of the community. Are we truly children of God? What does it mean to be authentically Christian? While positions may have hardened in opposition, beneath those stances was doubtless an abundance of uncertainty. The task of the author's community was to come to some greater clarity and certainty as to who it was. Those responsible for the publication of this epistle were pastorally sensitive to that need, and we see that sensitivity expressed in chap. 3.

The section is comprised of three parts. The first (vv. 1-3) addresses the general question of the origin and destiny of the children of God. The second (vv. 4-18) contrasts the life of the children of God with those whose allegiance is to that opposed to God. The third (vv. 19-24) speaks to the need for assurance that the allegiance of the community lies with God and to the need for moral righteousness. Laced through the three sections is the golden thread for which 1 John is best known—love. Children of God owe their origin to God's love (v. 1); it is love of others that characterizes their lives (v. 18); and that love is rooted in what God wills for the community (v. 23).

The Origin and Destiny of the Children of God (3:1-3)

The first three verses move through the three dimensions of time—past, present, and future. In the *past* lies the origin of the community—its adoption as children by God's love (v. 1a). In the *present* that community stands over against a hostile "world" (vv. 1b-2a). In the *future* lies its maturation as the family of God (vv. 2b-3).

1a—See has the force of both a cognitive consideration and a sensual perception. The **love** of which the author speaks is an established fact to be seen in the community's life, but it is also such an amazing reality that it must be pondered again and again. **What** expresses "both quantity and quality, thus, how much love and what amazing love" (Brown, *Epistles*, p. 387). For **love** (*aga-*

pē) cf. 2:5 above, and for **Father** cf. 1:2 above. **Has given us** translates a verb in the perfect tense indicating an action of the past—an accomplished fact. The **love** that creates the family of God is entirely a gift, and not a result of any virtue or preexisting character in the lives of persons. Here our author overcomes what sometimes in the Fourth Gospel appears as a gnostic feature: believers have their origin in some selected group of humans (e.g., 10:1-26). **That** translates *hina*, suggesting a connection of cause and effect: "in order that."

For **children of God** (*tekna theou*) cf. 2:13 above. This is the first use of *tekna* for **children,** and it is always used in 1 John in connection with **God** or the devil (cf. 3:2, 10; 5:2). This is in contrast to the Greek *teknion* ("little child"), the word used by our author to address the readers (2:1, 12, 28; 3:7, 18; 4:4; 5:21). This use of two different words for children is characteristic of the Fourth Gospel, as well (cf. John 1:12; 8:39; 11:52; and contrast 13:33, where *teknion* ["little child"] is used as it is in 1 John). Our author saves *teknon* ("child") for the fundamental relationship humans have which defines their identity, so that, in the typical Johannine dualism, one's parentage is either divine or evil. This notion of "extrahuman" parentage expresses the conviction of a basic allegiance and orientation which shapes personality and behavior. It is rooted in the OT images of Israel as children of Yahweh (e.g., Hos. 11:1), but is more seriously shaped by the Johannine tradition that the revelation of God forms a new divine family among humans (cf. 2:29 above). The idea is like that of Paul's (e.g., Gal. 3:26; 4:1-7; Rom. 8:14-17). **Called** once again suggests that the believers' divine parentage is dependent upon God's action, and not their inherent nature. God's act of calling out this new family is an established fact: **and so we are.** Not only is the community called by this name; it expresses its true nature. The notion implied is like that of justification. The believers are called children by God, and that means they *are* what God declares them to be, even though the imperative—to *be* what God has declared they are—still follows (e.g., 2:15).

1b—Attention shifts now from the origin of the community in

God's love to its present relationship to others outside the church—**the world** (cf. 2:2 above). "World" (Greek, *kosmos*) is used here in its classical Johannine sense as the realm of unbelief hostile to the community (e.g., John 15:18-19). **The reason why** is, literally, "for this reason," but the antecedent of "this" is not clear. Presumably it points forward to the assertion that **the world . . . did not know him.** For **know** cf. 2:3. It is used here in the sense of acknowledgment. Since the realm of unbelief has not acknowledged God in Christ, it cannot acknowledge Christians for what they are, namely, children of God. **Him** is again ambiguous, as pronouns often are from the pen of this author, and again the distinction between Christ and God as the antecedent matters little. The community finds itself set within a hostile environment, because others do not believe. Most likely, the author wants to imply the identification of the separatists with the world.

2—For **beloved** cf. 2:7 above. The author reasserts the point of v. 1a (cf. above) but with the emphasis on the **now,** so that he can point on toward the future maturation of the community. The Christians stand with one foot in the present and one in the future, affirming God's gifts and presence now but looking toward a fulfillment of God's work in their lives. That future is mysterious, however. For **appear** cf. 2:8. The reference is to the final revelation of Christ in the parousia. While the author wants to maintain the mystery of that last day, the fundamental expectation is known. **We know** expresses the confidence of faith (cf. 2:20 above). **He appears** may also be translated "it appears." But the difference hardly matters, since the sense is the eschaton.

Like him raises two issues: First, is the **him** Christ or God? Second, in what sense does the author mean that the Christian can expect to be **like** Christ or God? On the first question, it is impossible to determine the precise intent of the author, but the hint at the parousia in "he appears" (compare 2:28) tips the scales slightly in favor of Christ. **See him as he is** would, in that case, mean seeing Christ in his full glory with his present hiddenness removed.

74

The second question is no less easily answered. We may eliminate any sense of a divinization of the believers, since the concept of children of God preserves the distinction between the parent and the offspring in a Hebraic sense. But a notion of the glorification of the believers is a basic Johannine concept (John 17:22), although here it loses the strongly realized sense which it has in the gospel. If, in the Gospel of John, glory means, above all, the divine presence, then what the author has in mind is the believers' immersion in God's presence, even as Christ and the divine presence are one. The vision is that of an intimate, immediate relationship with God, not unlike that pictured in Revelation 21. This expectation that the readers will see Christ "as he is" is a promise that their doubts and uncertainties will ultimately be overcome; the implication is that the author's view of Christ will then be confirmed over against that of the separatists. One striking thing about this vision of the last day is how it postpones much of the affirmation of the Fourth Gospel to the distant future. What the fourth evangelist affirmed as a present reality, or the experience of believers immediately upon their death (cf. John 14:1-3; 17:22-23), is now fitted into a more traditional futuristic (and even apocalyptic) scheme.

3—The future expectation now becomes the basis of an exhortation, leading the thought toward vv. 4-10. **Every one who thus hopes** (*pas ho echōn tēn elpida tautēn*) is literally, "every one who has this hope." This is the only use of the noun **hope** in 1 John. The verb is used in 2 John 12 and 3 John 14, but without theological content (cf. John 5:45). **Hope** was not a major theological motif of the Johannine community, and only our author's use of a futuristic eschatology occasions its appearance here. **In him** and **as he is** are ambiguous. If our suggestion that Christ is the antecedent of the third person pronouns in v. 2b is sound, it follows that it is he who is in mind in this verse as well.

Purifies himself: This is the sole use of this verb in the Johannine epistles, and it is used only once in the Fourth Gospel, where it refers to Jewish practices of purification (11:55). (For the use of the related word, *hagios*, "holy," cf. 2:20.) It is sometimes employed elsewhere in the NT for the moral imperative (e.g., James 4:8; 1 Peter 1:22), but it is never elsewhere used to describe Christ. We must ask what the author means by the purity attributed to Christ and urged upon his readers. The controlling thought is the moral purity the author believes is required of Christians. The emphasis on morality found throughout 1 John— a morality not demonstrated to the author's satisfaction by the separatists—is here conceived of in basic Jewish cultic terms. **Purifies himself,** then, means to rid oneself of all those actions and attitudes which are inappropriate to one who lives in a saving relationship with Christ. It is the human's responsibility to prepare oneself for the eschatological day when Christians are made to be "as he is" and when they are immersed in the divine presence. The purity attributed to Christ, it follows, is a moral purity, and here the author implies the sinless perfection of Christ (a position made explicit in v. 5a below) which is found elsewhere in the NT literature of the last quarter of the first century (e.g., Heb. 4:15).

The Christians' stance is rooted in the experience of the past, standing in a present situation of conflict as a result of their view of that past, and propelled with hope into a future, which in turn places upon them demands for their present lives. In responding to the crisis of faith within the community this writer appeals to memory, suffering, and hope—all as an effort to nurture confidence while prodding the readers to live out what God has declared them to be.

Children of God Love; Children of the Devil Hate (3:4-18)

This section divides itself into two interrelated parts: vv. 4-10 and 11-18. A carefully conceived structure is evident in at least the first of the two parts. Verses 4-10 are made up of a pair of chiastic patterns. The center of each (marked with an asterisk) is an affirmation of the work of Christ.

4-6   Sin is lawlessness (4).
          *Christ has taken away sin (5).

Abiding in him means not sinning (6).
(Stated in the affirmative, then the negative.)
7-10 Doing right constitutes righteousness (7).
Sinners are of the devil (8a).
*Christ has destroyed the works of the devil (8b).
Those born of God (children of God) do not sin (9).
Lives show parentage—divine or evil (10).

Verse 4 is restated in an affirmative way in v. 6, with "abides in him" contrasted with lawlessness. The distinction is illuminated by appeal to Christ's atonement for sin. In v. 7 the structure shifts, but the point remains the same. "Doing right" (v. 7) parallels its negative in v. 10, "whoever does not do right." "Of the devil" (v. 8a) corresponds to its opposite in v. 9, "born of God." The two pairs of parallels are hinged again with the work of Christ stated in v. 8b. The impact is a tight exploration of the opposition between righteousness and evil.

Verses 11-18 betray a less artistic structure. The unifying theme is concrete love. The theme is announced in v. 11 and summarized in different words in v. 18, producing closures around the subject. The illustration of the Cain and Abel incident (v. 12) is followed by its point: Love of others is expression of life as opposed to death (v. 14), while hatred of others expresses the spirit of murder (v. 15). That contrast is picked up in the first of two statements about what it means to love—to lay down one's life for another (v. 16) and giving generously to those in need (v. 17). Verse 13 appears to be a parenthetical comment.

It immediately appears that these two subparts are welded together both in content and form. "Love of his brother" (v. 10b) uses the catchword *love*, picked up in v. 11b. As the work of Christ appears at the center of vv. 4-10 (vv. 5 and 8b), so it is used in v. 16. Finally, the word *abide* ties the parts together by its recurrence throughout the section—vv. 6, 9, 14, 15, and 17.

The general message of these verses is that the Christian is one whose life is distinguished by a moral quality comprised of love and freedom from sin. This is contrasted with unrighteousness and sin. At the heart of the argument is the division of humanity into "two families" (Holden, p. 89)—the children of God who love and the children of the devil who hate.[16]

4—Throughout this section, for **sin** and the claim that the Christian does not **sin**, cf. 1:8 above. **Commits sin** is, literally, "doing sin" (cf. 2:29 above, "does right"). **Lawlessness** brings into focus the view of the separatists, who (we gather) held to the view that their Christian faith elevated them above any moral imperative. We may conjecture that it was their view that life in relationship with Christ rendered earthly questions of morality insignificant. Whether their view of Christ was that of a pure spirit (cf. 2:22 above and 4:2 below) and whether that view persuaded them that only purely spiritual matters (and hence not physical concerns for relationships with other humans) were important is a matter of speculation. But at least it would seem that such gnostic views of a later time are anticipated in the perspective of the separatists (as they are represented to us here). Our author categorically equates all sin with this anomian (lawless) stance, a bit of simplistic hyperbole at worst, and a blurring of two views of perfectionism (cf. Introduction, p. 22) at best. That some form of anomianism (lawlessness) troubled early Christianity is widely attested in the NT in different strata of the literature. Paul fought against it (e.g., 1 Cor. 5:9-20; 2 Cor. 6:14); Matthew's community seems to have been troubled by it (7:23; 13:41; 24:12; cf. 5:17-20); and James may have been written to counteract an interpretation of Pauline thought which was without moral content (2:17). The separatists may have shared the thought of others in the first-century church who attached little, if any, importance to moral righteousness.

Lawlessness may also be used here in a technical apocalyptic sense. An early Christian apocalyptic scheme conceived of the onslaught of evil at the last day in terms of lawlessness (e.g., 2 Thess. 2:3-8). The apocalyptic motifs employed by our author those whose parentage lies with the devil, and the faithful members of the author's community are the children of God. It seems clear from his exhortations that he believes humans established their parentage by their response to the work of God in Christ. The thought of v. 7b is repeated in the negative, **whoever does not do right.** As a transition to vv. 11-15, the lack of **love** is paralleled to the failure to do **right,** for this author finds righteousness expressed most vividly in love.

In vv. 4-10 the author has again hammered at the point that authentic faith issues forth in righteous living. The message is grounded in soteriology—the saving work of Christ (vv. 5 and 8b). The cross means, among other things, that the human is freed for a life of righteousness and from a life alienated from God (i.e., sin). Furthermore, the cross means that humans have opportunity to be made children of God, if they choose to believe. Like the fourth evangelist, this author poses the alternatives dualistically—one is either a child of God or of the devil.

11—In vv. 11-15 love is contrasted to murder. Verse 11 announces the theme of vv. 11-18, and that theme is reiterated in v. 18: Mutual love within the community of faith. For **message** cf. 1:5 above. For **from the beginning** cf. 1:1. Here it refers to the origin of the reader's life of faith. For **you have heard** cf. 1:1. Now, however, it is the gospel which the reader (**you**) has **heard.** The point is the author's insistence that the theme of community **love** is not a new one introduced to combat the separatists, but one which was an integral part of the gospel message the community has always valued and proclaimed. **Love one another** is a stylistic variation of "love his brother" (cf. 2:10 and 3:10 above) and is used four additional times (3:23; 4:7, 11, 12) always with *agapaō* (the Greek verb *love*). It is obviously rooted in John 13:34; 15:12, 17. That the injunction to love is limited to the Christian community is characteristic of the Johannine tradition (contrast Matt. 5:43-44) and reflects its sectarian origins (however, cf. note 19).

12a—A negative illustration is introduced and love is contrasted with **murder.** The allusion to **Cain** is the only explicit reference

(e.g., 2:18-23, 28; 4:1, 17; 5:19) make it credible that the scheme of the last days known to him contained the figure of the "lawless one" not unlike the deutero-Pauline vision expressed in 2 Thessalonians.

5—**You know** appeals to the unquestioned basic beliefs of the readers. **Appeared** refers to the historical life of Jesus (cf. 1:2 above). **To take away sins** was the purpose of the historical revelation of God in Christ. This is the only use in the Johannine epistles of the Greek verb *airein* (**to take away**) to refer to the removal of sin, but it echoes John 1:29. It is surely another instance of our author's concept of atonement (cf. 1:7, 9; 2:2 above and 4:10 below). He uses a variety of verbs to express Christ's effect on sin, however ("forgive," 1:9; 2:12; "destroy," 3:8; "expiate," 2:2; 4:10; "cleanse," 1:9; cf. Brown, *Epistles*, p. 203), which suggests that he is searching for images to express a fundamental conviction that the reality of sin is overcome in the cross. But the cultic sacrificial orientation is reflected in the last part of v. 5. That Christ was himself without **sin** is important in the imagery of the sacrifice offered to God which would atone for sin (e.g., Leviticus 4 and 1 Peter 1:19). On Christ's sinlessness cf. v. 3 above.

6—The author now draws the conclusion of his assertions of vv. 4 and 5: The Christian does not sin. For **abides in him** cf. 2:6 above. **Seen him or known him** here has the sense of having a saving relationship with Christ. **Seen** is problematic, for the author surely does not mean a physical perception of the historical Jesus. "To see" here means to comprehend and appropriate in a "spiritual" sense, just as "to know" is used metaphorically to mean "to live in a relationship."

Here the author has stated his conviction that the Christian life-style is one that is sinless. This would seem to contradict both his assertion in 1:10 and 2:11 that Christians are not without sin and his discussion in 5:16 of types of sin. Several explanations of this contradiction have been proposed, the most popular being the suggestion that in 3:4 and 6 what is in view is sin as a way of life, as opposed to the other passages where reference is to past sinful acts and occasional lapses (cf. Brown, *Epistles*, pp. 412-415 for a discussion of the variety of interpretations). While there is much to commend this view, the explanation proposed in the Introduction §4 seems more reasonable. In the light of that view, the author has in mind here a basic sin of unbelief (cf. Bogart). The Christian cannot, then, sin in the sense of disbelief, for by definition one who "abides in him" and "has seen" and "known him" is one who believes. The contradictory statements, however, further document the assumption that the author is working from fragments of homilies delivered at different times and addressed to different situations.

7—The second subpart of vv. 4-10 asserts that Christian living requires righteousness. For **little children** cf. 2:1 above. For **deceive** cf. 2:26 above. **Right** and **righteous** in Greek are respectively *dikaiosynē* and *dikaios,* and can be translated "justice" and "just." Righteousness is clearly reflected in behavior. There is a polemic implied here against those who would claim that righteousness resides in some relationship with God without reference to the quality of life that relationship produces—a view of the separatists. **As he is righteous** may appeal to God's or Christ's fundamental righteousness. But in either case the sanction for the author's assertion that righteousness is reflected in behavior lies in divine precedent—God and Christ have *acted* righteously.

8a—In contrast to the origin of righteousness in divine precedent, **sin** has its origin in the **devil.** The RSV loses the parallelism between vv. 7 and 8a. In the Greek, v. 7 reads, "the one doing righteousness," and v. 8a, "the one doing sin." **Of the devil** is literally "out of the devil" and denotes origin, life orientation (cf. John 8:44). Our author uses the term **devil** (*ho diabolos*) only four times, all in the scope of vv. 8-10 (cf. the use of "evil one" in 2:13-14; 3:12; and 5:18-19). It denotes the opposition to God, and was sometimes used in the LXX to translate the Hebrew word *Satan* (e.g., Job 1:16). The author implies that those who **sin** are children of evil, just as those who do righteousness are children of God (cf. John 8:31-47). **Has sinned from the beginning** perhaps refers to any one of the several Jewish myths of the origin of Satan

in disobedience to God (e.g., *Life of Adam and Eve,* Vita 12-16). **Has sinned,** however, is in the present tense in the Greek, suggesting that continued disobedience is characteristic of th opponent of God.

8b—In this sentence the author once again refers to the effect of the work of Christ (cf. v. 5 above). **The reason** is literally "int this" (*eis touto*). **Appeared** is a reference to the historical Jesu as in v. 5. **Son of God** is used seven times in this document (here 4:15; 5:5, 10, 12, 13, 20) and is a stylistic variation of the more fre quent title, "Son," and, specifically, "his Son" (e.g., 5:9-10). T **destroy** (*lysē*) can also be rendered "to loose." It means to fre humans from the power of evil. Here the author invokes a slight different concept of atonement which centers in the objecti forces of opposition to God.[17]

9—As those who sin have their roots in the devil, so now th author asserts that those **born of God** do not **sin.** For **born God** cf. 2:29 above. The thought is a repetition of v. 6 (cf. above and the same concept of sin as unbelief is assumed. **God's natu** in the Greek is "his seed" (*sperma autou*), and is the only use the expression in 1 John. It is reminiscent, however, of John 8: and 37 which speak of the "seed of Abraham." *Sperma* may me "offspring" or the "seed" which begets offspring. In the conte the latter meaning seems more likely—God has implanted Christians that which makes them his children (cf. John 1:1 For **abides** cf. 2:6 and 10 above. The consequence of this is th humans are made to be children of God and hence incapable sin in the sense of total unbelief.

10—The author brings to its conclusion the structure begun v. 7 and essentially repeats the thought of that verse. The "sp itual parentage" of a person is revealed in the quality of his her life. **May be seen** is, more accurately, "shown" (*phaner* For **children of God** cf. 3:1 above. For **children of the devil** v. 8 above. Now the author borders on a division of human into two camps—those whose origin is with the creator God a those who are related to evil. But his point is less anthropologi than ethical; and, above all, it is polemical. The separatists to the OT in 1 John, but the story in Gen. 4:1-16 is used by several NT writers (e.g., Jude 11). It was a fairly frequent subject of Jewish discussion and speculation in the first century, as the works of Philo suggest (e.g., *Migration of Abraham*). **Cain who was of the evil one** means that Cain's "spiritual parentage" was with that opposed to God. (*The Apocalypse of Abraham* 24:5 makes a similar point.) **Brother** (*adelphon*) in this context means blood brother, but subtly suggests the spiritual sibling the author refers to so frequently in the expression "love his brother" (e.g., v. 10).

12b—The dramatic question posed here is best rendered, "and for the sake of what . . .?" The author's interest in the Cain and Abel story is simply to show that one's deeds betray one's basic roots in a simple dualistic fashion—**evil** or good. The **righteous** quality of Abel is a frequent NT allusion (e.g., Matt. 23:35 and Heb. 1:4). Does the author imply that Cain represents the separatists and Abel the faithful of the community?

13—This verse intrudes as a parenthetical comment which recalls the discussion in 3:2 (for **world** cf. the comments there). For **hate** cf. 2:9 and 11 above. If the **world** represents those aligned with evil, it is no wonder that its attitude toward the Christian is hatred. The verse recalls John 15:18 and 17:14 and reflects a sectarian mentality which is not entirely appropriate for the time 1 John was written. For our author the separatists are now playing the role of "the world."

14—The argument is picked up again, and the point of the Cain illustration is now made. **We know** is once again the assertion of the certainty of the community (cf. 3:2 above). **Passed** is, literally, "we have (been) removed." Cain's murderous deeds are now symbolized in **death** (*thanatos*). The author uses this word only here and in 5:16-17. It does not carry all of the theological import of Pauline usage (e.g., Rom. 6:23) but does function, in this instance, as a kind of suprahuman metaphor for the powers of evil. **Life** is the more common Johannine metaphor for salvation (e.g., John 1:4). **Because** implies that human salvation is the result of works of **love.** But we should be careful not to read a whole doctrine of soteriology into the author's words. The purpose is to insist that community love is the necessary manifestation of a redeeming relationship with God. **We know** that we are saved **because** of the quality of our relationship with one another. The *because* clause gives the basis for the community's certainty. The last sentence of the verse drives home the polemic against the separatists, who do not express love for the community. They are in relationship with the forces opposed to God. Notice the way **abides** is used here to suggest that, as one is a child either of God or the devil, so one either "abides" in God or in God's opposition.

15—This verse continues the point of the allusion to Cain. For **hates** cf. 2:9 above. **Murderer** is the rare Greek word *anthrō-poktonos*, found only here and John 8:44 in the NT and seldom in classical Greek. In John 8:44 it is applied to the devil, and means that the forces of opposition to God are intent upon depriving humanity of "life" in the sense of salvation. The author issues a stern judgment: anyone who does not share the mutual love of the community is the equivalent of the devil. With this he adds to the growing lists of indictments against the separatists. They cannot, therefore, have **eternal life** (cf. 1:2 above). For **abiding** cf. 2:6 and 10 above. This conclusion may be a direct attack upon the claims of the opponents to have eternal life. **You know** is still another instance of the author's attempt to build the argument on basic assumptions he shares with the readers and to nurture a confidence among them.

16—In vv. 16 and 17 the author gives two examples of what it means to **love.** Having announced the theme in v. 11 and given a negative illustration in vv. 12, 14-15, attention is now turned to examples of love in sacrificial deed. The first is the example of surrendering **life** for the sake of the community, and it is founded on an allusion to Christ's sacrifice. The source of our knowledge of what love is and how it functions is found in none other than the cross. Christian love is not born from within the character of the individual but originates in Christ's act. The reference to the cross reflects the language of the Fourth Gospel (e.g., 10:15 and

15:13). **Life** (*psychē,* "soul") suggests the whole being—person—as opposed to physical life (*bios*). With Christ's sacrifice as the example, the injunction follows. **Ought** is used three times in 1 John (here, 2:6, and 4:11) and in each case in connection with a divine example. The imperative is rooted in the divine act after which it is to be modeled. The contrast between the murder of Abel by his brother and surrendering one's life for others is subtle and effective.

17—The second example is less lofty: the simple sharing of wealth with the needy. But the two examples are cleverly tied together, for the word translated **goods** is *bios,* another word for "life." In this case it means "livelihood." If Christians ought to surrender their lives for others in the community, then, too, they ought to give up their livelihood for the same (cf. 2:16 where the relative value of worldly life is stated). One who is not willing to share worldly goods with a needy member of the community cannot have **God's love . . . in him. Closes his heart** means to withhold compassion, to shut oneself off from his or her inner being. The positive example of surrendering life is here followed by the example of surrendering material possessions, stated in the negative.

18—The theme which v. 11 announced is repeated, with the additional force of *how* the Christian is to love. For **little children** cf. 2:1 above. **Love** is to be done **in deed and truth** as opposed to **word and speech.** The parallelism is not perfect and is not intended to be. The former pair means actions which arise from **truth** in the Johannine sense of the revelation of God in Christ (cf. 1:6 above). It is not simple sincerity which is urged, but actions which imitate divine deed, just as v. 16 exhorted. The latter pair is essentially synonymous, however, meaning verbalization of loving intentions. One is tempted to see here still another blast at the author's opponents, accusing them of talking about love but not acting it out. Our author's view is not far from that of Paul, who spoke of "faith active in love" (Gal. 5:6).

In 3:4-18 we have seen our author move from a condemnation of a pretense of Christian life which shunned morality to the epitomization of authentic Christian life in active, sacrificial love. Underlying the discussion are a number of assumptions: (1) Human deeds betray basic allegiances and "spiritual parentage." (2) A genuine Christian existence gives expression to itself in righteousness and love. The polemic and the dualistic presuppositions of the author lead to the posing of the alternatives in a radical polarity (love/hate, children of God/children of the devil). But the author here nurtures a sense of importance of the moral dimension of life and raises the question of the basic roots from which a life draws its nourishment.

The Assurance of Keeping God's Commandments (3:19-24)

The author has tended to move back and forth between exhortation and assurance, as if wanting to stir the readers with the imperative while still encouraging them with positive reenforcement. In this section the latter becomes prominent.

The unit is enclosed by two sentences beginning with "By this we (shall) know" (vv. 19 and 24a). Between these instructions for coming to certainty there are two issues discussed: Reassurance of the heart (vv. 19b-21) and keeping the commandments (vv. 22-24a). Within the discussion of each there is a "catchword" progression of thought. Within vv. 19b-21 first the word *heart* and then the word *condemn* seem to move the logic of the thought along. In vv. 22-24 it is the word *commandment* which links the discussion. Beyond this stylistic unity and the general theme of confidence there is little structure to be found in this section. The Greek of the section is decidely confusing; there are numerous textual variants which result from scribal efforts to improve the clarity of the passage.

19-20—The general meaning of vv. 19-21 is widely disputed, and the solution lies beyond the reaches of grammar, structure, and theology. The best we can endeavor here is to present an interpretation which makes some sense of the verses as a declaration of assurance, in spite of the fact that some have seen the passage in terms of threat rather than assurance (cf. Brown, *Epistles*, pp. 453-460).

By this we shall know is problematic because of the fact that the antecedent of **this** is far from clear, some holding that the antecedent lies in the previous verse, others in what follows. It is best perhaps to seek it in v. 20, "God is greater than our hearts." It is in that affirmation that the author hopes to find certainty in times of doubt. **Of the truth** is literally, "out of the truth," meaning having one's basic orientation in truth. For **truth** cf. 1:6 above. **Reassure** means "to set at ease or rest" (cf. Haas, De Jonge, and Swellengrebel, p. 95). **Hearts** may refer to thought, emotions, or something like conscience, but in any case has to do with the inner life of the individual and his or her state of being. **Whenever** renders *hoti*, usually translated "because" or "that." In this case it is not clear what sense it should be assigned, but it seems to suggest the occasion described in the clause "when our hearts condemn us." Hence, the author is saying that when our inner being judges against us, we are reassured by the fact that **God is greater than our hearts and he knows everything.** The sense of this obscure sentence is that God's grace and forgiveness exceed our inner state of being and God's knowledge measures us with greater generosity than we can measure ourselves.

Is the reassurance spoken of in v. 19a found in the assertion of God's nature stated in v. 20 or in the fulfillment of the admonition to love in deed expressed in v. 18? The latter is a viable interpretation, but the former renders the section more meaningful.

21—The sense of this verse seems to be that, if we find correction for our own condemnation in God's nature as stated in v. 20, then **our hearts do not condemn us** and **we have confidence before God. Confidence** (*parrēsian*) is used three other times in 1 John—twice in reference to eschatological events (2:28 and 4:17) and once in the context of the certainty of answered prayer (5:14). Its use here seems to span those two contexts, with the theme of condemnation in v. 20 suggesting eschatological judgment and that of answered prayer arising in v. 22. Our structural analysis above, however, implies that the **confidence** spoken of here has to do with the condemnation of the heart, while only suggesting the theme which opens vv. 22-24.

22—This verse makes the transition to the second major part of vv. 19-24. It begins with the restatement of the promise of the Johannine Jesus that God grants what is requested in prayer (e.g., 14:13, 14; 15:7, 16—cf. 5:14-16 below). The **because** (Greek, *hoti*) clause is, however, troublesome, for it seems to suggest that faithfulness to the **commandments** and pleasing God are reasons for God's granting of prayer requests. There is no need to try to read a full theology out of this briefly stated promise. The statements in the **because** clause are conditions in one sense: the requests of one who is faithful and pleasing to God are precisely those which God *can*, without exception, grant. Just as the extravagant promise of the Johannine Jesus is qualified by expressions such as "in my name" (14:13 and 14) and "if you remain in me" (15:7), so this author claims that requests arising from within the context of faithfulness are bound to be the kind God can grant. For **commandments** cf. 2:3 above. **Do what pleases him** seems to be synonymous with **keep his commandments.**

23—The **commandments** must now be specified, and they are two in number. **Believe in the name of his Son Jesus Christ** and **love one another.** The first is, literally, "believe the name of his Son"—without the preposition "in." This author uses the verb **believe** (*pisteuein*) in a variety of constructions (compare, e.g, 5:1 and 5:10) without any apparent variation of meaning. However, it is clear that for our author belief had taken on a certain creedal quality with the result that the present expression implies an acceptance of the creedal statement that Jesus was the Christ and God's Son. There is possibly a suggestion here that the separatists cannot make this confession (cf. 2:22 above). **Name** means person (cf. 5:13). The commandments are both rooted in the Gospel of John (e.g., 14:1 and 13:34; cf. 3:11 above) and reflect the Johannine tradition. **Just as he has commanded** seems redundant, but is added for exhortatory effect. The **he** would seem to be God, given the antecedent of **his** in the phrase **his son Jesus,** even though it was Jesus who gave this **commandment.** This is still another instance of the way in which the author moves freely between God and Jesus in the use of the personal pronouns.

24a—Faithfulness to the **commandments** assures one of a reciprocal relationship between the Christian and God. For **abide** cf. 2:6 and 10 above. This is the first time the author has used the reciprocal form of the abiding—**in him and he in them** (literally, "in him abides and he in him"!)—but he repeats it in 4:13, 15, 16. It is an expression drawn from the Fourth Gospel (e.g., 15:5) and denotes mutual intimacy. Keeping the commandments is closely linked with the relationship of God and the Christian, for it is the relationship which motivates faithfulness, and faithfulness which nutures the relationship.

24b—The author closes the section with another **by this we know** (cf. v. 19). Now he is concerned, however, to answer the question of how one can be confident of the reciprocal relationship just mentioned. **This** points to the **Spirit**. The Greek reads, "out of the Spirit" (*ek tou pneumatos*), which puzzles interpreters who want to take the author's prepositions with great seriousness. *Ek* is used to suggest that the certainty of the relationship with God arises from the presence of the Spirit. This is the first use of *Spirit* in 1 John, although there will be seven other occurrences (4:1, 2, 3, 6, 13; 5:7, 8). The author's fundamental concept of the Spirit is that of the presence of God made possible through the revelation in Christ and contingent upon him. It is shaped by the Paraclete passages of the Gospel of John, in particular 14:16-17 and 16:8-13.

In this confusing section the author has offered assurance that inner personal condemnation need not be final, that God answers the requests of those who stand in a faithful relationship with him, and that an intimate relationship with God is given through the Spirit. It is the purpose of this section to offer confidence to a community torn asunder by schism, and it points the reader to what can be held with certainty amid the many uncertainties of life. Within the larger section of chap. 3 the author has offered the reader self-identity through defining the origin and destiny of Christians and distinguishing them from what he regards as distorters of the gospel. The larger unit offers the modern reader a glimpse of the importance of Christian self-definition and demarcation of the source of assurance for enduring crisis.

■ The Spirit of Truth and the Spirit of Error (4:1-6)

The association of "the Spirit" (3:24) with "every spirit" (4:1) occasioned the placement here of a discussion of the discernment of the source of every claim to spiritual leadership. The structure of the section is simple, but it is another example of our author's use of "closures." The section begins with reference to "every spirit" (v. 1) and concludes with mention of "the spirit of truth and the spirit of error" (v. 6). The pastoral purpose of the section is to provide the readers with a warning against spirit-led authorities and give them a way of discerning between those to be trusted and those to be held in suspicion. To this is added a dualistic understanding of the Christian in the world (vv. 4-6a).

The Necessity to Identify Spirits (4:1)

1—The author begins by warning against gullibility. **Spirit** (*pneumati*) here seems to mean those extrahuman beings who were believed to reside in the world, some of which were evil and some good. This multitude of spiritual beings is amply attested in other NT writers (e.g., Gal. 4:3,9) and in the literature from Qumran (e.g., *Thanksgiving Hymns* 3:18). The author has in mind not simply the anthropological spirits, but supernatural beings who inspire and lead humans. The verb **test** (*dokimazete*) occurs nowhere else in Johannine literature; it means "to put to the test," "examine," or "prove." The idea of discerning the identity of a spirit is found elsewhere in the NT (e.g., 1 Cor. 12:10). The necessity for doing so is expressed in the last clause of the verse. **False prophets** are mentioned a number of times in the NT (e.g., Luke 6:26) and in the later church (e.g., Did. 11:7-12), but only here in the Johannine literature. Often they are asso-

(e.g., 2:18-23, 28; 4:1, 17; 5:19) make it credible that the scheme of the last days known to him contained the figure of the "lawless one" not unlike the deutero-Pauline vision expressed in 2 Thessalonians.

5—**You know** appeals to the unquestioned basic beliefs of the readers. **Appeared** refers to the historical life of Jesus (cf. 1:2 above). **To take away sins** was the purpose of the historical revelation of God in Christ. This is the only use in the Johannine epistles of the Greek verb *airein* (**to take away**) to refer to the removal of sin, but it echoes John 1:29. It is surely another instance of our author's concept of atonement (cf. 1:7, 9; 2:2 above and 4:10 below). He uses a variety of verbs to express Christ's effect on sin, however ("forgive," 1:9; 2:12; "destroy," 3:8; "expiate," 2:2; 4:10; "cleanse," 1:9; cf. Brown, *Epistles*, p. 203), which suggests that he is searching for images to express a fundamental conviction that the reality of sin is overcome in the cross. But the cultic sacrificial orientation is reflected in the last part of v. 5. That Christ was himself without **sin** is important in the imagery of the sacrifice offered to God which would atone for sin (e.g., Leviticus 4 and 1 Peter 1:19). On Christ's sinlessness cf. v. 3 above.

6—The author now draws the conclusion of his assertions of vv. 4 and 5: The Christian does not sin. For **abides in him** cf. 2:6 above. **Seen him or known him** here has the sense of having a saving relationship with Christ. **Seen** is problematic, for the author surely does not mean a physical perception of the historical Jesus. "To see" here means to comprehend and appropriate in a "spiritual" sense, just as "to know" is used metaphorically to mean "to live in a relationship."

Here the author has stated his conviction that the Christian life-style is one that is sinless. This would seem to contradict both his assertion in 1:10 and 2:11 that Christians are not without sin and his discussion in 5:16 of types of sin. Several explanations of this contradiction have been proposed, the most popular being the suggestion that in 3:4 and 6 what is in view is sin as a way of life, as opposed to the other passages where reference is to past sinful acts and occasional lapses (cf. Brown, *Epistles,* pp. 412-415 for a discussion of the variety of interpretations). While there is much to commend this view, the explanation proposed in the Introduction §4 seems more reasonable. In the light of that view, the author has in mind here a basic sin of unbelief (cf. Bogart). The Christian cannot, then, sin in the sense of disbelief, for by definition one who "abides in him" and "has seen" and "known him" is one who believes. The contradictory statements, however, further document the assumption that the author is working from fragments of homilies delivered at different times and addressed to different situations.

7—The second subpart of vv. 4-10 asserts that Christian living requires righteousness. For **little children** cf. 2:1 above. For **deceive** cf. 2:26 above. **Right** and **righteous** in Greek are respectively *dikaiosynē* and *dikaios,* and can be translated "justice" and "just." Righteousness is clearly reflected in behavior. There is a polemic implied here against those who would claim that righteousness resides in some relationship with God without reference to the quality of life that relationship produces—a view of the separatists. **As he is righteous** may appeal to God's or Christ's fundamental righteousness. But in either case the sanction for the author's assertion that righteousness is reflected in behavior lies in divine precedent—God and Christ have *acted* righteously.

8a—In contrast to the origin of righteousness in divine precedent, **sin** has its origin in the **devil.** The RSV loses the parallelism between vv. 7 and 8a. In the Greek, v. 7 reads, "the one doing righteousness," and v. 8a, "the one doing sin." **Of the devil** is literally "out of the devil" and denotes origin, life orientation (cf. John 8:44). Our author uses the term **devil** (*ho diabolos*) only four times, all in the scope of vv. 8-10 (cf. the use of "evil one" in 2:13-14; 3:12; and 5:18-19). It denotes the opposition to God, and was sometimes used in the LXX to translate the Hebrew word *Satan* (e.g., Job 1:16). The author implies that those who **sin** are children of evil, just as those who do righteousness are children of God (cf. John 8:31-47). **Has sinned from the beginning** perhaps refers to any one of the several Jewish myths of the origin of Satan in disobedience to God (e.g., *Life of Adam and Eve*, Vita 12–16). **Has sinned,** however, is in the present tense in the Greek, suggesting that continued disobedience is characteristic of the opponent of God.

8b—In this sentence the author once again refers to the effects of the work of Christ (cf. v. 5 above). **The reason** is literally "into this" (*eis touto*). **Appeared** is a reference to the historical Jesus, as in v. 5. **Son of God** is used seven times in this document (here, 4:15; 5:5, 10, 12, 13, 20) and is a stylistic variation of the more frequent title, "Son," and, specifically, "his Son" (e.g., 5:9-10). **To destroy** (*lysē*) can also be rendered "to loose." It means to free humans from the power of evil. Here the author invokes a slightly different concept of atonement which centers in the objective forces of opposition to God. [17]

9—As those who sin have their roots in the devil, so now the author asserts that those **born of God** do not **sin.** For **born of God** cf. 2:29 above. The thought is a repetition of v. 6 (cf. above), and the same concept of sin as unbelief is assumed. **God's nature** in the Greek is "his seed" (*sperma autou*), and is the only use of the expression in 1 John. It is reminiscent, however, of John 8:33 and 37 which speak of the "seed of Abraham." *Sperma* may mean "offspring" or the "seed" which begets offspring. In the context the latter meaning seems more likely—God has implanted in Christians that which makes them his children (cf. John 1:12). For **abides** cf. 2:6 and 10 above. The consequence of this is that humans are made to be children of God and hence incapable of sin in the sense of total unbelief.

10—The author brings to its conclusion the structure begun in v. 7 and essentially repeats the thought of that verse. The "spiritual parentage" of a person is revealed in the quality of his or her life. **May be seen** is, more accurately, "shown" (*phanera*). For **children of God** cf. 3:1 above. For **children of the devil** cf. v. 8 above. Now the author borders on a division of humanity into two camps—those whose origin is with the creator God and those who are related to evil. But his point is less anthropological than ethical; and, above all, it is polemical. The separatists are those whose parentage lies with the devil, and the faithful members of the author's community are the children of God. It seems clear from his exhortations that he believes humans established their parentage by their response to the work of God in Christ. The thought of v. 7b is repeated in the negative, **whoever does not do right.** As a transition to vv. 11-15, the lack of **love** is paralleled to the failure to do **right,** for this author finds righteousness expressed most vividly in love.

In vv. 4-10 the author has again hammered at the point that authentic faith issues forth in righteous living. The message is grounded in soteriology—the saving work of Christ (vv. 5 and 8b). The cross means, among other things, that the human is freed for a life of righteousness and from a life alienated from God (i.e., sin). Furthermore, the cross means that humans have opportunity to be made children of God, if they choose to believe. Like the fourth evangelist, this author poses the alternatives dualistically—one is either a child of God or of the devil.

11—In vv. 11-15 love is contrasted to murder. Verse 11 announces the theme of vv. 11-18, and that theme is reiterated in v. 18: Mutual love within the community of faith. For **message** cf. 1:5 above. For **from the beginning** cf. 1:1. Here it refers to the origin of the reader's life of faith. For **you have heard** cf. 1:1. Now, however, it is the gospel which the reader (**you**) has **heard.** The point is the author's insistence that the theme of community **love** is not a new one introduced to combat the separatists, but one which was an integral part of the gospel message the community has always valued and proclaimed. **Love one another** is a stylistic variation of "love his brother" (cf. 2:10 and 3:10 above) and is used four additional times (3:23; 4:7, 11, 12) always with *agapaō* (the Greek verb *love*). It is obviously rooted in John 13:34; 15:12, 17. That the injunction to love is limited to the Christian community is characteristic of the Johannine tradition (contrast Matt. 5:43-44) and reflects its sectarian origins (however, cf. note 19).

12a—A negative illustration is introduced and love is contrasted with **murder.** The allusion to **Cain** is the only explicit reference to the OT in 1 John, but the story in Gen. 4:1-16 is used by several NT writers (e.g., Jude 11). It was a fairly frequent subject of Jewish discussion and speculation in the first century, as the works of Philo suggest (e.g., *Migration of Abraham*). **Cain who was of the evil one** means that Cain's "spiritual parentage" was with that opposed to God. (*The Apocalypse of Abraham* 24:5 makes a similar point.) **Brother** (*adelphon*) in this context means blood brother, but subtly suggests the spiritual sibling the author refers to so frequently in the expression "love his brother" (e.g., v. 10).

12b—The dramatic question posed here is best rendered, "and for the sake of what . . .?" The author's interest in the Cain and Abel story is simply to show that one's deeds betray one's basic roots in a simple dualistic fashion—**evil** or good. The **righteous** quality of Abel is a frequent NT allusion (e.g., Matt. 23:35 and Heb. 1:4). Does the author imply that Cain represents the separatists and Abel the faithful of the community?

13—This verse intrudes as a parenthetical comment which recalls the discussion in 3:2 (for **world** cf. the comments there). For **hate** cf. 2:9 and 11 above. If the **world** represents those aligned with evil, it is no wonder that its attitude toward the Christian is hatred. The verse recalls John 15:18 and 17:14 and reflects a sectarian mentality which is not entirely appropriate for the time 1 John was written. For our author the separatists are now playing the role of "the world."

14—The argument is picked up again, and the point of the Cain illustration is now made. **We know** is once again the assertion of the certainty of the community (cf. 3:2 above). **Passed** is, literally, "we have (been) removed." Cain's murderous deeds are now symbolized in **death** (*thanatos*). The author uses this word only here and in 5:16-17. It does not carry all of the theological import of Pauline usage (e.g., Rom. 6:23) but does function, in this instance, as a kind of suprahuman metaphor for the powers of evil. **Life** is the more common Johannine metaphor for salvation (e.g., John 1:4). **Because** implies that human salvation is the result of works of **love.** But we should be careful not to read a whole doctrine of soteriology into the author's words. The purpose is to insist that community love is the necessary manifestation of a redeeming relationship with God. **We know** that we are saved **because** of the quality of our relationship with one another. The *because* clause gives the basis for the community's certainty. The last sentence of the verse drives home the polemic against the separatists, who do not express love for the community. They are in relationship with the forces opposed to God. Notice the way **abides** is used here to suggest that, as one is a child either of God or the devil, so one either "abides" in God or in God's opposition.

15—This verse continues the point of the allusion to Cain. For **hates** cf. 2:9 above. **Murderer** is the rare Greek word *anthrō-poktonos,* found only here and John 8:44 in the NT and seldom in classical Greek. In John 8:44 it is ˻˼˻ˈ˼ed to the devil, and means that the forces of opposition to God are intent upon depriving humanity of "life" in the sense of salvation. The author issues a stern judgment: anyone who does not share the mutual love of the community is the equivalent of the devil. With this he adds to the growing lists of indictments against the separatists. They cannot, therefore, have **eternal life** (cf. 1:2 above). For **abiding** cf. 2:6 and 10 above. This conclusion may be a direct attack upon the claims of the opponents to have eternal life. **You know** is still another instance of the author's attempt to build the argument on basic assumptions he shares with the readers and to nurture a confidence among them.

16—In vv. 16 and 17 the author gives two examples of what it means to **love.** Having announced the theme in v. 11 and given a negative illustration in vv. 12, 14-15, attention is now turned to examples of love in sacrificial deed. The first is the example of surrendering **life** for the sake of the community, and it is founded on an allusion to Christ's sacrifice. The source of our knowledge of what love is and how it functions is found in none other than the cross. Christian love is not born from within the character of the individual but originates in Christ's act. The reference to the cross reflects the language of the Fourth Gospel (e.g., 10:15 and

15:13). **Life** (*psyche*, "soul") suggests the whole being—person—as opposed to physical life (*bios*). With Christ's sacrifice as the example, the injunction follows. **Ought** is used three times in 1 John (here, 2:6, and 4:11) and in each case in connection with a divine example. The imperative is rooted in the divine act after which it is to be modeled. The contrast between the murder of Abel by his brother and surrendering one's life for others is subtle and effective.

17—The second example is less lofty: the simple sharing of wealth with the needy. But the two examples are cleverly tied together, for the word translated **goods** is *bios,* another word for "life." In this case it means "livelihood." If Christians ought to surrender their lives for others in the community, then, too, they ought to give up their livelihood for the same (cf. 2:16 where the relative value of worldly life is stated). One who is not willing to share worldly goods with a needy member of the community cannot have **God's love . . . in him. Closes his heart** means to withhold compassion, to shut oneself off from his or her inner being. The positive example of surrendering life is here followed by the example of surrendering material possessions, stated in the negative.

18—The theme which v. 11 announced is repeated, with the additional force of *how* the Christian is to love. For **little children** cf. 2:1 above. **Love** is to be done **in deed and truth** as opposed to **word and speech.** The parallelism is not perfect and is not intended to be. The former pair means actions which arise from **truth** in the Johannine sense of the revelation of God in Christ (cf. 1:6 above). It is not simple sincerity which is urged, but actions which imitate divine deed, just as v. 16 exhorted. The latter pair is essentially synonymous, however, meaning verbalization of loving intentions. One is tempted to see here still another blast at the author's opponents, accusing them of talking about love but not acting it out. Our author's view is not far from that of Paul, who spoke of "faith active in love" (Gal. 5:6).

In 3:4-18 we have seen our author move from a condemnation of a pretense of Christian life which shunned morality to the epitomization of authentic Christian life in active, sacrificial love. Underlying the discussion are a number of assumptions: (1) Human deeds betray basic allegiances and "spiritual parentage." (2) A genuine Christian existence gives expression to itself in righteousness and love. The polemic and the dualistic presuppositions of the author lead to the posing of the alternatives in a radical polarity (love/hate, children of God/children of the devil). But the author here nurtures a sense of importance of the moral dimension of life and raises the question of the basic roots from which a life draws its nourishment.

The Assurance of Keeping God's Commandments (3:19-24)

The author has tended to move back and forth between exhortation and assurance, as if wanting to stir the readers with the imperative while still encouraging them with positive reenforcement. In this section the latter becomes prominent.

The unit is enclosed by two sentences beginning with "By this we (shall) know" (vv. 19 and 24a). Between these instructions for coming to certainty there are two issues discussed: Reassurance of the heart (vv. 19b-21) and keeping the commandments (vv. 22-24a). Within the discussion of each there is a "catchword" progression of thought. Within vv. 19b-21 first the word *heart* and then the word *condemn* seem to move the logic of the thought along. In vv. 22-24 it is the word *commandment* which links the discussion. Beyond this stylistic unity and the general theme of confidence there is little structure to be found in this section. The Greek of the section is decidely confusing; there are numerous textual variants which result from scribal efforts to improve the clarity of the passage.

19-20—The general meaning of vv. 19-21 is widely disputed, and the solution lies beyond the reaches of grammar, structure, and theology. The best we can endeavor here is to present an interpretation which makes some sense of the verses as a declaration of assurance, in spite of the fact that some have seen the passage in terms of threat rather than assurance (cf. Brown, *Epistles*, pp. 453-460).

By this we shall know is problematic because of the fact that the antecedent of **this** is far from clear, some holding that the antecedent lies in the previous verse, others in what follows. It is best perhaps to seek it in v. 20, "God is greater than our hearts." It is in that affirmation that the author hopes to find certainty in times of doubt. **Of the truth** is literally, "out of the truth," meaning having one's basic orientation in truth. For **truth** cf. 1:6 above. **Reassure** means "to set at ease or rest" (cf. Haas, De Jonge, and Swellengrebel, p. 95). **Hearts** may refer to thought, emotions, or something like conscience, but in any case has to do with the inner life of the individual and his or her state of being. **Whenever** renders *hoti*, usually translated "because" or "that." In this case it is not clear what sense it should be assigned, but it seems to suggest the occasion described in the clause "when our hearts condemn us." Hence, the author is saying that when our inner being judges against us, we are reassured by the fact that **God is greater than our hearts and he knows everything.** The sense of this obscure sentence is that God's grace and forgiveness exceed our inner state of being and God's knowledge measures us with greater generosity than we can measure ourselves.

Is the reassurance spoken of in v. 19a found in the assertion of God's nature stated in v. 20 or in the fulfillment of the admonition to love in deed expressed in v. 18? The latter is a viable interpretation, but the former renders the section more meaningful.

21—The sense of this verse seems to be that, if we find correction for our own condemnation in God's nature as stated in v. 20, then **our hearts do not condemn us** and **we have confidence before God. Confidence** (*parrēsian*) is used three other times in 1 John—twice in reference to eschatological events (2:28 and 4:17) and once in the context of the certainty of answered prayer (5:14). Its use here seems to span those two contexts, with the theme of condemnation in v. 20 suggesting eschatological judgment and that of answered prayer arising in v. 22. Our structural analysis above, however, implies that the **confidence** spoken of here has to do with the condemnation of the heart, while only suggesting the theme which opens vv. 22-24.

22—This verse makes the transition to the second major part of vv. 19-24. It begins with the restatement of the promise of the Johannine Jesus that God grants what is requested in prayer (e.g., 14:13, 14; 15:7, 16—cf. 5:14-16 below). The **because** (Greek, *hoti*) clause is, however, troublesome, for it seems to suggest that faithfulness to the **commandments** and pleasing God are reasons for God's granting of prayer requests. There is no need to try to read a full theology out of this briefly stated promise. The statements in the **because** clause are conditions in one sense: the requests of one who is faithful and pleasing to God are precisely those which God *can*, without exception, grant. Just as the extravagant promise of the Johannine Jesus is qualified by expressions such as "in my name" (14:13 and 14) and "if you remain in me" (15:7), so this author claims that requests arising from within the context of faithfulness are bound to be the kind God can grant. For **commandments** cf. 2:3 above. **Do what pleases him** seems to be synonymous with **keep his commandments.**

23—The **commandments** must now be specified, and they are two in number. **Believe in the name of his Son Jesus Christ** and **love one another.** The first is, literally, "believe the name of his Son"—without the preposition "in." This author uses the verb **believe** (*pisteuein*) in a variety of constructions (compare, e.g, 5:1 and 5:10) without any apparent variation of meaning. However, it is clear that for our author belief had taken on a certain creedal quality with the result that the present expression implies an acceptance of the creedal statement that Jesus was the Christ and God's Son. There is possibly a suggestion here that the separatists cannot make this confession (cf. 2:22 above). **Name** means person (cf. 5:13). The commandments are both rooted in the Gospel of John (e.g., 14:1 and 13:34; cf. 3:11 above) and reflect the Johannine tradition. **Just as he has commanded** seems redundant, but is added for exhortatory effect. The **he** would seem to be God, given the antecedent of **his** in the phrase **his son Jesus,** even though it was Jesus who gave this **commandment.** This is still another instance of the way in which the author moves freely between God and Jesus in the use of the personal pronouns.

24a—Faithfulness to the **commandments** assures one of a reciprocal relationship between the Christian and God. For **abide** cf. 2:6 and 10 above. This is the first time the author has used the reciprocal form of the abiding—**in him and he in them** (literally, "in him abides and he in him"!)—but he repeats it in 4:13, 15, 16. It is an expression drawn from the Fourth Gospel (e.g., 15:5) and denotes mutual intimacy. Keeping the commandments is closely linked with the relationship of God and the Christian, for it is the relationship which motivates faithfulness, and faithfulness which nutures the relationship.

24b—The author closes the section with another **by this we know** (cf. v. 19). Now he is concerned, however, to answer the question of how one can be confident of the reciprocal relationship just mentioned. **This** points to the **Spirit.** The Greek reads, "out of the Spirit" (*ek tou pneumatos*), which puzzles interpreters who want to take the author's prepositions with great seriousness. *Ek* is used to suggest that the certainty of the relationship with God arises from the presence of the Spirit. This is the first use of *Spirit* in 1 John, although there will be seven other occurrences (4:1, 2, 3, 6, 13; 5:7, 8). The author's fundamental concept of the Spirit is that of the presence of God made possible through the revelation in Christ and contingent upon him. It is shaped by the Paraclete passages of the Gospel of John, in particular 14:16-17 and 16:8-13.

In this confusing section the author has offered assurance that inner personal condemnation need not be final, that God answers the requests of those who stand in a faithful relationship with him, and that an intimate relationship with God is given through the Spirit. It is the purpose of this section to offer confidence to a community torn asunder by schism, and it points the reader to what can be held with certainty amid the many uncertainties of life. Within the larger section of chap. 3 the author has offered the reader self-identity through defining the origin and destiny of Christians and distinguishing them from what he regards as distorters of the gospel. The larger unit offers the modern reader a glimpse of the importance of Christian self-definition and demarcation of the source of assurance for enduring crisis.

■ The Spirit of Truth and the Spirit of Error (4:1-6)

The association of "the Spirit" (3:24) with "every spirit" (4:1) occasioned the placement here of a discussion of the discernment of the source of every claim to spiritual leadership. The structure of the section is simple, but it is another example of our author's use of "closures." The section begins with reference to "every spirit" (v. 1) and concludes with mention of "the spirit of truth and the spirit of error" (v. 6). The pastoral purpose of the section is to provide the readers with a warning against spirit-led authorities and give them a way of discerning between those to be trusted and those to be held in suspicion. To this is added a dualistic understanding of the Christian in the world (vv. 4-6a).

The Necessity to Identify Spirits (4:1)

1—The author begins by warning against gullibility. **Spirit** (*pneumati*) here seems to mean those extrahuman beings who were believed to reside in the world, some of which were evil and some good. This multitude of spiritual beings is amply attested in other NT writers (e.g., Gal. 4:3,9) and in the literature from Qumran (e.g., *Thanksgiving Hymns* 3:18). The author has in mind not simply the anthropological spirits, but supernatural beings who inspire and lead humans. The verb **test** (*dokimazete*) occurs nowhere else in Johannine literature; it means "to put to the test," "examine," or "prove." The idea of discerning the identity of a spirit is found elsewhere in the NT (e.g., 1 Cor. 12:10). The necessity for doing so is expressed in the last clause of the verse. **False prophets** are mentioned a number of times in the NT (e.g., Luke 6:26) and in the later church (e.g., Did. 11:7-12), but only here in the Johannine literature. Often they are associated with eschatological (apocalyptic?) contexts (e.g., Mark 13:22; Rev. 16:13; 19:20; 20:10). It is likely that the reality of these pseudo-spokespersons for God was part of the author's understanding of the eschatological drama (cf. 2:18 above). **World** (*kosmon*) is used here in a neutral sense of the society, in contrast to its pejorative use in vv. 4-5.

It is clear that our author held that the crisis of the schism in his community meant that the faithful were subject to misguidance by those who claimed to be directed by the Spirit. It is the separatists who are the false prophets and the bearers of spirits of which the faithful should beware.

The Identity of the Spirit of God and of the Antichrist (4:2-3)

In this section the author gives the criterion by which the readers might distinguish the presence of the Spirit of God from the inspiration of evil spirits. It is comprised of an affirmative and then a negative statement.

2—**This** refers to the confession later in the verse. The phrase **Spirit of God** occurs nowhere else in Johannine literature. **Jesus Christ has come in the flesh** is one of several possible translations, but in every case the sense remains nearly the same. The expression recalls John 1:14. **Is of God** repeats the exact phrase used in v. 1 and means "having its origin and inspiration from God."

3—The author now states the opposite of what has just been said. But **Jesus** is now apparently used as shorthand for the longer statement in v. 2, "Jesus Christ has come in the flesh." This would seem to suggest that the historical name *Jesus* had come to stand for the earthly, fleshly appearance of the Messiah (cf. 2:22 above). Such a denial of the human life of Christ is labeled **antichrist.** (The Greek does not contain the words **spirit of.**) For **antichrist** cf. 2:18 above; note the similar argument in 2:18-23. As in 2:18, the author assumes that the readers are familiar with the idea of the **antichrist** as part of the scheme of the last days. Such a view would not have come from the community's tradition but from apocalyptic influence. **Now it is in the world** reflects the author's view that the last days were imminent (again, cf. 2:18 above). **World** is again used in a neutral sense, as in v. 1.

This constitutes the clearest evidence in 1 John that the separatists held to a Christology which denied the humanity of Christ and contended instead for some view of a purely spiritual appearance of the Messiah. For this author such a view was of dire importance, for he calls it the work of the antichrist and the eschatological liar (2:22). Our author believed that such a central doctrine was of ultimate importance and not merely a matter of intellectual preference.

Being of God and Being of the World (4:4-6)

To the necessity and means of discerning false and true spiritual inspiration the author appends a word of assurance. The purpose of these verses is to facilitate the readers' sense of distinction between themselves and the separatists. The section adopts a dualistic perspective which poses the believers and the "world" in diametrical opposition. In doing so, the author has fallen back on his readers' understanding of their tradition, for such a dualism permeates the Fourth Gospel (e.g., 17:16). The unit moves through three steps: (1) assuring the readers that they are strengthened by God, who is greater than the forces of opposition (v. 4), (2) distinguishing them from those who find their support in the opposition (v. 5), and (3) affirming that those who accept the gospel are in relationship with God (v. 6). The discussion is tied together with the recurrence of the word *world* used in a negative sense.

4—For **little children** cf. 2:12 above. For **of God** cf. 3:10 and its synonym, "children of God," in the comments there. **Overcome** might better be rendered "conquered" or "vanquished." It is this verb that is used so frequently in Revelation of the Lamb and the faithful martyrs (some 15 times, e.g., 2:7,11,17; 17:14), and it is found on the lips of the Johannine Jesus (16:33). It is the latter which shapes our author's use of it: as Christ has conquered the **world,** so have the believers (2:13,14; 5:4,5). **World**

(*kosmos*) now appears in its pejorative sense as the realm of unbelief and evil, as opposed to its purely descriptive sense in v. 1. **Them** refers to those of v. 3 who are identified with the antichrist. The reason for the believers' conquest of evil forces is that **God's** power is with them and exceeds that of the opposition. **He who is in you** refers to **God** or the divine Spirit. **He who is in the world** must be an allusion to the personification of the forces of evil (cf. 5:19 below). In 1 John **God** three times is said to be **greater** (3:20; 5:9; and here).

5-6a—These two verses constitute a parallel comparison of the separatists and the members of the community. The contrast includes four points: (1) origin/allegiance, (2) the nature of what is said, (3) who listens, and (4) who does not listen. Regarding (1) the opponents are **of the world** and the believers **of God** (repeated from v. 4). Regarding (2) only what the opponents **say** is characterized, again with the expression **of the world.** Regarding (3) the **world listens** to the opponents, while those who **know God** listen to the believers. Regarding (4) only those who do **not listen** to the believers are characterized—**he who is not of God. Listen** (*akouei*) means receptive hearing of the speaker's message. **Therefore** suggests that the speakers' position is determined by their basic affiliation. **Knows** in v. 6a suggests correct intellectual knowledge (in our author's view) but also carries something of its Hebraic sense of intimate relationship. The distinction between being **of the world** and **of God** may have the ring of gnostic predestination, and the Johannine tradition contributed to the later gnostic view of this matter. But here the expressions are descriptive of the affiliations persons have made for themselves.

6b—The section concludes by returning to the basic point of the distinction between spirits (cf. v. 1 above). But again the use of **this** is problematic. In this case the construction is the only occurrence in 1 John of the Greek *ek toutou* ("from this"), rather than the usual *en toutō* ("by this" or "in this"). It obviously refers back, but to how much of vv. 1-6a? While the confession in v. 2 is the primary criterion for distinguishing between spirits, it is likely the author has the whole of vv. 1-6a in mind. Still, how vv.

4-6a contribute to the separation of the spirits is not entirely clear. **The spirit of truth and the spirit of error** sounds very much like the language and conceptuality of the Qumran community, where a dualistic view of the end-time prevailed (e.g., 1QS 3:15). **The spirit of truth** is drawn from the Fourth Gospel, where this title is used of the Paraclete (14:17; 15:26; 16:13). In that document **truth** is used in the sense of the revelation of God in Christ, although one wonders whether "truth" for the present author has not come to mean right doctrine. **Spirit of error,** on the other hand, is used nowhere else in the NT. On **error** cf. "deceive" in 1:8 and 2:26 above. The title is drawn by our author from his view that the eschatological drama involved the forces of evil deceiving humans into error (cf. 2:22).

The section oversimplifies the struggle of the church into a dualistic scheme where truth is exclusively on one side and error on the other. Such oversimplification and polemic mentality are typical of a community under stress. In such conditions humans are prone to defend themselves by polarizing the situation. It provides certainty and comfort. But with all the weaknesses of the message of this section it does affirm the continuing necessity for Christians to "test" what they hear proclaimed and to inquire concerning its spiritual source. The sectarian "us-against-them" mentality is fraught with perils, but it exemplifies the way in which Christian commitment separates the believers from others.

■ God's Love and the Believers' Love (4:7—5:5)

The author here takes up love as the central theme, after having alluded to it a number of times (e.g., 2:5,15; 3:1,16,17). The statement "We know the spirit of truth . . ." (4:6) occasions the transition to the new section—"knows God" (4:7b). This unit gives expression to three principles and one imperative. The principles are: (1) God is love (4:8 and 16); (2) God's love evokes human love (4:9-10,19); and (3) abiding in love is abiding in God (4:16). The imperative is simply that the Christians should love one another

(4:7, 11, 21; 5:1), for such love gives expression to a relationship with God (4:20).

The section moves through three parts: 4:7-12; 4:13-18; and 4:19—5:5. It is striking that some form of the word *love* (*agapē*) appears 33 times in these 21 verses!

God's Love Evokes Human Love (4:7-12)

The first part announces the author's central imperative (v. 7a), and articulates the first two principles stated above (vv. 8-10). After having established that love is of God and hence is the test of the relationship one has with God (vv. 7b-8), the Christ event is interpreted as an expression of God's love (vv. 9-10) and its ethical point is driven home (v. 11). Love is then stated to be God's presence (v. 12). It is instructive that once again the author has constructed a three-part paragraph with the soteriological meaning of Christ constituting the middle member (cf. 3:4-10 above). In these verses the author is near his best as a poet, for they betray an intentionally balanced construction, with the word *love* appearing in the first line of each of the strophes.

7a—The main message of 4:7—5:5 is announced here. The imperative is comprised in Greek of only three words, *agapētoi agapōmen allēlous* (**Beloved, let us love one another**). For **beloved** cf. 2:7 above. For **love one another** cf. 3:11. It is this imperative the author intends to lay down through his theological reflection. The first theological rationale for the imperative is that **love** stems from **God** and takes its origins there (cf. 3:9 above). Genuine human love always has its roots in God.

7b-8—Now the logical conclusion for human behavior is drawn from the theological point just made. The loving person stands in a relationship with God. The conclusion is stated in a positive and then negative (incomplete) parallelism. **Born of** and **knows God** are expressions of the saved, Christian relationship (cf. 2:29; 3:9; and 2:13 above). An alliteration appears in the Greek with the words **born** (*gegennētai*) and **knows** (*ginōskei*). Verse 8a states the same point in the negative, but **know** is now in the aorist tense, while in v. 7b the verb is present. The sense is, "has never known God," emphasizing the negative and suggesting that the separatists have never had a Christian relationship with God. The theological principle stated at the end of v. 7a is repeated for emphasis.

9a—The Christ event is for the author the supreme expression of the nature of God as love. Both vv. 9 and 10 begin with the expression **in this** (*en toutō*). **This** points ahead to the next phrase in each case. **Was made manifest** is one of our author's favorite expressions for the historical revelation in Jesus (cf. 1:2 and "appeared" in 3:8 above). **The love of God** is ambiguous. Does it mean the human love of God, or God's love of humans? While either is defensible (Christ revealed how God loves humans; or, how humans are to love God), the latter is more likely intended here (a subjective rather than an objective genitive). **Among us** translates *en hēmin* and raises several questions. The first is whether the Greek phrase is to be taken with the verb, **manifested,** or the noun, **love.** The RSV favors the former, although the Greek word order places *en hēmin* after **the love of God,** making possible the translation, "the love of God for us." A majority of commentators, however, favors the RSV here. But *en hēmin* can denote either locale (as in the RSV) or purpose (as in TEV, "his love for us"). Verse 16 would suggest that the second is closer to the author's intended meaning.

9b—The way this **love** was revealed is stated in v. 9b. The clause repeats the thought of the Fourth Gospel (e.g., 3:16). **Sent** is one of the fourth evangelist's favorite expressions for the mission of Jesus (*apostellō;* e.g., 3:17; 5:38; 6:29; it is used interchangeably with *pempō*). The verb (always *apostellō*) is used three times in 1 John (here, v. 10, and v. 14). For our author it is a traditional term, the meaning of which is the divine intentionality of the Christ event. **His only Son** is also uniquely Johannine language. **Only Son** (*monogenēs*) is used of Christ only here and in John (1:14, 18; 3:16, 18). For the fourth evangelist it stated the uniqueness of Christ's sonship in relationship with that of Israel and the Christians. Again, for the author of 1 John it is a traditional term with the same meaning but without the intensity it had for his predecessor. **Into the world** echoes John 3:16. For **world** (Greek, *kosmos*) cf. 3:13 and 17 above. Here it is probably used in a neutral way—the realm of humans. **So that we might live through him** states the redemptive purpose of the Christ event. This is the only use of the verb **live** in 1 John, although it is relatively common in the Fourth Gospel (e.g., 5:25) as a symbol for the benefits of Christ's revelation. Our author uses "life" as a symbol of salvation (cf. 1:1 above) and intends the verb in the same sense. Christian life is authentic, genuine existence, as it was intended by God. **Through him** means as a consequence of his life. In the language of his tradition, the author has declared that it was God's love which motivated the redemptive act of the revelation in Christ.

10—Next, the theological foundations for the life of **love** are further expanded. For **in this** cf. v. 9a above. Part of what constitutes love is its imitative nature. Human love only mimics the divine act. The purpose of the verse is to establish the priority of God's love over Christians' love. The first verb, **loved,** is in the perfect tense, while the second is an aorist; thus: "Not that we have loved God, but that he once concretely loved us." The synonym for that concrete act of divine love is **sent his Son to be the expiation for our sins.** For **sent** cf. v. 9b above. For **expiation** cf. 2:2 above. The initiative lies with God. Love is not a human virtue but a mere reflection of God's specific, historical act for the benefit of humanity.

11—The ethical imperative drawn from the soteriological center of the argument is here stated. The human response is shaped by the divine action. The first verb, **loved,** is again in the aorist tense, to suggest the historical charcter of God's love. For **ought** cf. 3:16 above. "God's love is his gift to us, but at the same time it is an obligation laid upon us" (Haas, De Jonge, and Swellengrebel, p. 109). From the indicative of what God has done arises an imperative for humans.

12—With this verse the argument shifts slightly, in order to make the point that God's presence is found in loving others. The first clause of the verse is drawn from the author's tradition (cf. John 1:18) and from OT interpretation (Exod. 33:18; Isa. 6:5). One might expect the author to have qualified this assertion, since the Johannine Jesus is made to claim that seeing him is seeing God (14:9), but our author is not thinking primarily of Christology here but of the ethical necessity of loving. Loving **one another** assures the Christian of God's presence. For **abides** cf. 2:6, 10 above. Loving one another is for our author both the expression of a saving relationship with God and an assurance that God is present. **His love is perfected in us** is somewhat confusing. The verb **perfected** is used four times in 1 John, all in connection with love (2:5, cf. above; here; 4:17; and 18). (The adjective, "perfect," is used once in 4:18, also in connection with the same subject.) **Perfected** here has the sense of bringing to maturation or completion, and not necessarily of freedom from fault. **His love** (*hē agapē autou*) may be an objective (our love of God) or a subjective genitive (God's love of us), and commentators divide evenly on the issue. While a case can be made for either, the logic of the section may favor a subjective genitive. In loving others Christians bring to completion the loving act of God in Christ. That redemptive plan is complete only when those who have been loved in Christ love one another.

The author has grounded his imperative in the historical Jesus and the meaning of that event. He has shown that divine love is concrete and redemptive and that it provides the basis for Christian love of one another. It has been effectively shown that Christian love is the inescapable conclusion to be drawn from divine love.

Confidence in God's Love (4:13-18)

These verses almost seem to be an illogical invasion of the progress of thought in 4:7—5:5, for they divert attention away from the imperative the author is exhorting. But it is typical of 1 John to mix the imperative with the note of assurance (cf. 3:19-24 above). While wanting to move his readers toward Christian behavior, the author wants always to affirm them in their present faith. Still, vv. 13-15 appear to be a parenthetical remark, since v. 16 argues on the basis of vv. 7-12, rather than on that of vv. 13-15. After vv. 13-15, however, the theme of assurance comes back to love as its central theme: abiding in God and abiding in love (v. 16) and the perfection of the believers' love (vv. 17-18).

13—This verse gives the basis of v. 12. How it is that God "abides" in us is answered by reference to the **Spirit. By this** refers ahead to the gift of the Spirit. **Know** here suggests certainty or confidence. The reciprocal relationship suggested by **we abide . . . in us** has been alluded to earlier, and there too it is the **Spirit** which makes the relationship possible (cf. 3:24 above). The word **gave** is in the perfect tense, suggesting an act in the past with enduring consequences.

14—For **seen and testify** cf. 1:1, 2 above. For **sent** cf. 4:9 above. The **we** in this case refers most probably to both the readers and the author, for the latter wishes to emphasize the ground for the readers' assurance. **Savior of the world** occurs only here in 1 John, as it occurs only once in the Gospel of John (4:42). Like the fourth evangelist, the author of 1 John does not use "save" as a metaphor for redemption. The title **Savior** may suggest Hellenistic influence (in the Gospel of John it is on the lips of Samaritans), but it is used of Yahweh in the Old Testament (e.g., Isa. 43:3 and 11). Here, however, it reflects the Johannine tradition.

15—This verse betrays a polemic against the separatists (cf. 2:22-23 above). For **Son of God** cf. 3:8 above. We may take it that **Jesus** stands as an abbreviation for the historical man, as opposed to the position of the separatists who seemed to qualify the fleshly appearance of **the Son of God** (cf. 4:3 above). For the reciprocal relationship, **God abides in him and he in God,** cf. 3:24 above. This appears to be a caveat against any reading of the author's words which might tend to minimize the importance of doctrinal stance. The relationship, of which the readers are assured in this section, is possible only for those who properly understand the revelation of God to have occurred in the historical man, Jesus.

16a—The argument returns to its center in **love. So** translates a simple *kai* ("and"). But here it does seem to mean that what follows in this verse is somehow based on what has been established in previous verses. The logical connection, however, is better between this verse and vv. 7-12 than between this verse and vv. 13-15. **We know and believe** is a unique expression for this document, although the author often uses **know** (either of two Greek words) to speak of the shared faith of the community (e.g., 3:2; 4:13). The two verbs are in this case in the perfect tense, "we have known and have believed," although no sharp distinction should be drawn between the perfect and aorist tenses in this case. They are merely stylistic variations. The pairing of "know and believe" is found in the Gospel of John several times (e.g., 6:69) and suggests the close relationship and even equivalence of the two in the mind of the evangelist. Our author relates the two in 5:13 in such a way as to imply that they are synonyms. However, **know** carries more of a sense of intellectual certitude than it does for the fourth evangelist. The assumption is that faith produces a certainty. **The love God has for us** is, literally, "the love God has in us" (cf. v. 9a above for the same kind of expression). Since the argument of the verse concerns abiding in love, the translation "in us" is preferable here.

16b—**God is love** repeats the statement of v. 8b (cf. above). The author's intent is less to describe the nature of God than to epitomize the meaning of God's actions among humans—the concern of vv. 9-11. For the thought that abiding in **love** means **God abides** in the believer cf. v. 12 above. Having claimed that loving one another assures us that **God abides** with the believer, the author in v. 15 expanded the "abiding relationship" to a reciprocal one, and now asserts that abiding in love means having that intimate reciprocal relationship. **Abides in love** means living a consistently caring life with regard to other members of the community (cf. John 15:9). For the reciprocal relationship cf. 3:24 above. Loving one another is evidence of a relationship with God.

17a—The argument now moves to the assurance of the perfection of the believers' love. **In this** here refers the reader back to the affirmations of the previous verse. In the relationship with God the perfection of **love** is given. For **perfected** cf. v. 12 above. **With us** is a strange expression, the precise meaning of which is not clear. Perhaps it means "among us in our actions toward one another." **That** translates *hina*, meaning "toward the end that." For **confidence for the day of judgment** cf. 2:28 and 3:21 above, where the same theme is discussed. **Day of judgment** is not used elsewhere in 1 John. In fact, this is the author's only use of either the noun *judgment* or the verb *judge*. The fourth evangelist showed little interest in the future, apocalyptic judgment and stressed instead the judgment that takes place in one's initial encounter with Christ. Our author adopts the apocalyptic scheme of the future judgment under the influence of extra-Johannine thought. The expression **day of judgment** is witnessed in Jewish (e.g., 4 Ezra 7:113) and Christian thought (Matt. 10:15; 11:22; 2 Peter 2:9; 3:7).

17b—The meaning of this last clause is obscure. It is literally, "because just as that one is also we are in this world." Who is the **he** ("that one")? The antecedent immediately at hand in v. 16 is God, but the logical antecedent is Christ, who is **in this world** in v. 9 (and we have seen how the author can move indiscriminately between God and Christ in the use of pronouns). Because Christ was in this world, the Christian can be confident about her or his life here. Christ's life in this world gives the believers a model for their lives in the midst of tension and difficulty.

18a—Jesus' model of a loving relationship with God leads to the assertion that **fear** has no place in **love**. This is the sole use of **fear** (*phobos*) in 1 John, and its use in the Gospel of John gives us no clue as to its meaning (e.g., 7:13; 19:38; 20:19). Here it seems to have to do with fear of judgment. Fear of God is a common OT theme (e.g., Isa. 59:19) and fear of the **punishment** of God is not uncommon (e.g., Mic. 7:17). The Greek is, literally, "fear is not in love." The **love** under consideration here is the believers' love of God and one another. **Perfect love** is not a love without fault, but one that has reached its maturity in a relationship with God (cf. 4:12 above). **Casts out** renders *exō ballei*, which means "to throw outside" (used in its literal sense in Luke 20:15 and Acts 7:58 and its metaphorical sense in John 12:31). The author does not mean to say that the loving Christian is free of all fear but only that he or she is not fearful of the judgment of God, a way of restating the point of v. 17.

18b—For translates *hoti*, which connects this clause with the one preceding. This indicates that **fear** of **punishment** is unnecessary where there is confidence in **love.** In the clause **fear has to do with punishment, has to do with** renders *echei*, meaning "has or holds." It may suggest several things about the relationship of fear and punishment, e.g., "fear contains punishment" or "fear is its own punishment." But the point of the author is that fear arises out of anticipation of one's destiny in the final judgment. The word translated **punishment** (*kolasin*) is used only here and in Matt. 25:46 ("eternal punishment"), but appears in Jewish literature in reference to both human injury (e.g., 4 Macc. 8:9) and divine retribution (2 Macc. 4:38). The one who is fearful of God's judgment has not reached maturity in love. The passage is a sensitive pastoral response to readers who are fearful, amid the crisis of the community, that they will be judged in error at the last day. The author assures them that if they attend to their loving relationships with others they need have no anxiety about the final verdict.

In this remarkable passage the readers have been assured of God's immediate presence in the love the community practices within itself. It is that love which nurtures a joyful anticipation of God's completion of the kingdom. If the people have responded to God's loving act in Christ by loving one another, they face God's assessment of them without dread.

Love among the Children of God (4:19—5:5)

The theme of love is explored still further in these verses, expanding what has already been said. The presupposition of the section is announced in 4:19. The discussion in 4:20—5:5 then pivots around "family language": "brother" (4:20,21), "commandment(s)" of the parent of the family (4:21; 5:2,3), "child"/ "children" (5:1,2), "parent" (5:1), "born of" (5:4), and "Son" (5:5). In 4:20—5:2 the argument that one cannot love God without loving others is made in the negative by calling those who do not love other Christians "liars" (4:20) and disobedient (4:21). It is then made in the affirmative by stating that children love their siblings (5:1) and are obedient to their parent (5:2). Verse 3 insists that loving one's parents means obeying them. There follows an appendix (5:4-5) on overcoming the world, which implies that proper faith assures the readers that they will rise above the troubles of their fractured and troubled communal life.

19—The argument of the earlier section (particularly vv. 9-11) is restated, to introduce the thesis that one only truly loves God by loving others. **We love** raises two questions: First, is it love of God or others that is intended? Given the argument that is to follow, both are probably in view. Second, the verb in Greek may be an exhortation ("let us love") or a description of fact ("we do love"). The latter seems the present intent of the author. **First** means here both prior in time and foremost in importance. For **loved** cf. v. 10 above. God's love enables human love, providing both its source and its motivation.

20—It is now denied that one can **love God** without loving others. For **if any one says** cf. 1:6,8,10 above. The language is polemical and aimed against those separatists, who (in the author's view) claim love of God but do not practice a caring attitude toward members of the community. For **hates** cf. 2:9 above. **Brother** means another Christian. For **liar** cf. 1:10 and 2:22 above. Here the term accuses the unloving Christian of a lack of integrity but also equates them with the eschatological antichrist figures. The charge of inconsistency is made in the second clause of the verse with a commonsense analogy. If persons cannot love a concrete historical being, how can they love an invisible, supernatural one? For not seeing **God** cf. 4:12 above.

21—Persons who claim to **love God** but do not **love** others not only lie, but also are disobedient. For **commandment** cf. 2:7 and

3:23 above. The author takes some liberties with the statement of the command here, for nowhere is it stated in this way (compare John 13:34; 15:12,17; 1 John 2:3-4; 3:22-24). Loving one another is never attached to loving God, as it is here, and **love his brother** is a free rendering of "love one another." Does the tradition of Jesus' summary of the Law (Mark 12:30-31) lie behind the author's thought?[18] **From him** refers to God (as scribal corrections attempted to clarify), even though the **commandment** is attributed to Jesus in the tradition (cf. 3:22 above).[19]

5:1—The argument now turns to the positive, having been condemnatory in 4:20-21, and another commonsense analogy is invoked: If you **love** your parents, you will also love your siblings. The polemical tone, however, is continued. For **every one . . . Christ** cf. 2:22 above. **Child of God** is literally, "has been born of God," for which cf. 2:29; 3:9; 4:7 above. Brown points out that all the uses of the word **believe** in 1 John have to do with Christology (*Epistles*, p. 534; cf. John 1:10-12). The author once again asserts his dogmatic position, which he understands the separatists to deny. With the assertion **everyone who loves . . . child,** the author is saying that love of God necessitates loving those who are children of God.

2—The positive argument is stated now in terms of loving and obeying **God. By this** refers ahead to the two following clauses, but the logic of the argument is difficult to discern. How is it that the certainty that **we love the children of God** is attained from **when . . . commandments?** The sense would seem to reverse what was just said in 4:20. There the evidence of love of God was found in loving others; here the certainty that we love others is derived from loving and obeying God! The point is that we can authentically love others only if that love has its source in our love of God and our concern to be faithful to the commandment. As *automatic* as communal love is when the relationship with God is sound, so believers can be assured that if their relationship with God is intact, their communal love is *genuine*. The implication is that there is a reciprocality between the two dimensions of Christian love—toward God and toward others. The author at this point has slipped from polemic to assurance.

3—One further step is necessary in the argument the author has been building, and that is to state the relationship between loving and obeying. The development of the argument leads one to think that **love of God** is an objective genitive (our love of God). Of what is love of God constituted? Foremost is obedience. **Keep** is used frequently in the Gospel of John (e.g., 14:15); it is a stylistic variation of "obey" (literally, "do") in the previous verse. **Burdensome** means a heavy weight (cf. Matt. 23:4, where the word is used of traditional interpretations of the Torah). How might the **commandments** be viewed as burdensome? One wonders if the separatists, who practiced a freedom of moral obligation (cf. 2:9-11 above), might have declared such obligations a burden from which Christ had freed them (cf. Matt. 11:30). For the Christian the commandments are no burden, because they are obeyed within the context of love, which allows one to obey out of joy and gratitude rather than obligation.

4—The tone of assurance sounded in v. 2 is continued now in what appears to be an appendage to the argument. It is connected to the argument, however, by **born of God** (cf. "child of God," 5:1 above). **Whatever** (Greek, *pan*) is neuter; this is strange, given the fact that the masculine has been used above (cf. *pas*, "every one," 5:1). This may be a generic use of the neuter to indicate inclusivity. For **overcomes** cf. 2:13,14; 4:4 above. For **the world** cf. 3:13 above, where it refers to the realm of unbelief, as here. **Victory** (Greek, *nikē*) is derived from the same word translated **overcomes** (Greek, *nika*). The RSV loses the alliteration of the Greek. **Faith** for our author is defined in the next verse. This is the only use of the noun **faith** in 1 John, and it does not appear in the Gospel of John. Its use hints at the fact that faith for this author is less a dynamic trust than a doctrinal stance (cf. v. 5 below). **The world** that is conquered is the unbelief represented in the separatists and their views.

5—The author now defines the faith just mentioned. **Jesus is the Son of God** means confession of the identity of the historical

man, Jesus, and God's Messiah—an identity the separatists seem
to have denied (cf. 2:22 above). The appendage on victory over
the world is clearly another strike at the author's opponents.

In 4:7—5:5 the author has explored the inextricable relationship between God's love of humanity and the believers' love of
one another. The latter is clearly grounded in the former. It is
God's love in Christ that initiates love and forever becomes the
source of authentic human love. The theological basis for the
argument is of primary importance, and we see the author's theological acumen here at its best. The purpose of the section is at
once exhortatory, polemical, and reassuring—a delicate and com-
plicated blending of purposes. Above all, once again we have
evidence of the pastoral sensitivities of the author, speaking as
he was to a readership in a peculiar situation. The section shows
us the way in which pastoral counsel arises from a theological and
Christological context. Our author was a pastoral theologian in
the best sense.

■ The Son and the Witnesses (5:6-12)

The insistence on the humanity of Christ has surfaced as one
of the major themes of the author's charge against the separatists
(cf. 2:22; 3:23; and 4:2 above). It now takes center stage once
again, linked with the motif of witness. The subject is associated
with the previous section by means of the mention of "Jesus . . .
the Son of God" in 5:5 and "Jesus Christ" in 5:6. The section 5:6-
12 is divided into three parts: The first announces the theme of
the section (v. 6), while the second attempts to support the humanity of Christ through the three witnesses (vv. 7-8). The third
part moves behind the three witnesses, as it were, to the witness
of God and its meaning for the believer (vv. 9-12). Without im-
posing upon the author a full sense of the doctrine of the Trinity,
it is to be observed that his argument begins with Christ (v. 6),
appeals to the Spirit (vv. 7-8), climaxes with God (vv. 9-11), and
concludes again with Christ (v. 12).

The Humanity of Christ (5:6)

6—**This is** has a polemical tone, announcing with confidence that **Jesus** was a human. **Who came** resounds with Johannine meaning, since the Johannine Jesus again and again speaks of his coming (e.g., John 5:43; 7:28; 8:42), and our author uses this expression of the advent of **Christ** in 4:2 as well as here. **By** (or through) **water and blood** (Greek, *di' hydatos kai haimatos*) suggests by its construction that the two nouns are viewed as a single entity. Textual variants here seem to be scribal efforts to harmonize this verse with the three witnesses in v. 8. For **Jesus Christ** cf. 2:22 above. **Not with . . . the blood** seems constructed for emphasis. The preposition here is *en* (**in**) instead of *dia* ("through") as in the first clause, and "in" is repeated before each of the nouns. But the meaning of the shift is not discernible. Each of the nouns, **water** and **blood,** is used here with the definite article, while the article is absent in the first occurrence of each in the earlier part of the verse. While commentators differ in their understandings of these variations between the two parts of the verse, it seems clear only that the author wants to add emphasis with the last half. **Only** translates *monon*, used by our author one other time—in 2:2.

What is the meaning of **water and blood?** Among the various interpretations, the one which arises most naturally from the context of the argument of 1 John is that they are references to the humanity of Christ. That they are linked with John 19:34 ("But one of the soldiers pierced his side with a spear, and at once there came out blood and water") is clear; the author invokes that passage to prove the fleshly reality of God's revelation in Jesus. The Gospel passage affirms the reality of the death of Jesus (cf. Kysar, *John,* pp. 291-292), and this author has used that affirmation and its logical extension that Christ was, therefore, fully human. That a reference to the sacraments is intended is reading too much into the symbolism. That a distinction between Jesus' baptism (**water**) and his death (**blood**) is intended is, however, likely.

What then is meant by the emphatic distinction **not with the water only but with the water and the blood?** Behind this lies the view of the separatists, but it is difficult to make out. This much is sure: the author is insisting on the death of Christ as a genuine part of his life, which means the opponents must have questioned that. If **the water only** represents their view, the most logical guess would be that they held to the reality of the Messiah's baptism, but not his death. If theirs was a docetic Christology, they might have contended that the Spirit descended upon the historical man Jesus at his baptism but was not a participant in the death of that man. Our author is affirming that the Messiah was indeed baptized (**came by water**) but also suffered death. The general thrust of the verse is, then, to insist upon the humanity of Christ from (at least) his baptism through his death.[20]

Three Witnesses to the Truth (5:7-8)

7—Now the author enumerates the evidence for his insistence on the humanity of Christ by calling forth witnesses. For **Spirit** cf. 3:24 and 4:2 above. For **the Spirit is the truth** cf. 4:6 above. **Witness,** in either its verbal or substantive form, is frequent in 1 John (sometimes translated "testify," e.g., 1:2) and plays an important role in the Gospel of John (e.g., 1:7; 5:31-39). Its meaning is "to speak on behalf of the truth." **Because** translates *hoti* and may mean that what follows is the content of the testimony of the Spirit or the reason for the Spirit's testimony. The latter is more likely, in the light of the argument of the context. How it is that the Spirit gives testimony is less clear. Is it an internal experience of the believer to which the author is appealing or some event in the history of the Johannine community? The answer lies in the community's sense of having been given the Spirit/Paraclete as promised by the Johannine Jesus (e.g., John 14:17). The testimony of the Spirit is less an internal, individualistic phenomenon than a corporate one. The author is appealing to the church's life together over the years as evidencing the truth of their conviction that the Christ was the historical Jesus.

It is at this point in the text that a textual variant, known as the "Johannine Comma," is found and has effected the versification. This textual variant seems to be an effort to elucidate the sense of vv. 7-8. It read, "in heaven, the Father, the Word, and the Holy Ghost; and these three are one. And there are three witnesses on earth" (translation by Haas, de Jonge, and Swellengrebel, p. 119). The reading has no support among the oldest and most trusted manuscripts, and is obviously a late scribal clarification. (Cf. Brown, *Epistles*, pp. 785-787.)

8—Now the **three witnesses** are brought together. The verse begins with another *hoti* ("because," "for"), which makes for a clumsy construction, since v. 7b also begins with this word. Perhaps here it has the sense of "indeed." To the testimony of the Spirit is added now the two nouns employed in v. 6, **the water and the blood** (cf. above). To substantiate the historical, human nature of the Christ the author appeals to Jesus' baptism, his death, and the work of the Spirit within the community. Efforts to find here allusion to the sacraments seem, again, unnecessary, especially in the light of the scarcity of sacramental language in 1 John.

In John 5:31-40 Jesus appeals to four **witnesses** in addition to his self-testimony: The Father, John the baptizer, the divine works given to Jesus to do, and Scriptures. I suggest that our author may have drawn upon this Gospel passage to formulate the argument of this verse. From the testimony of the baptizer he draws the witness of water (since John speaks of the Spirit descending upon Jesus, John 1:32); from "the works which the Father has granted me to accomplish" (John 5:36), the death of Jesus; and from the testimony of the Father (John 5:32 and 37), the witness of the Spirit (since the Spirit comes from the Father— John 14:16). These are adapted, however, to the author's peculiar interest in sanctioning the community's conviction regarding the humanity of Christ. **These three agree** is, literally, "the three into the one are" (*hoi treis eis to hen eisin*). There may be a reference here to Deut. 19:15 which speaks of the necessity of two or three witnesses to establish a case. The three merge into one to produce undeniable persuasion.

The Witness of God in the Son (5:9-12)

The argument of these verses is that none other than God has testified to the truth of Christ's humanity (v. 9), that belief is by definition acceptance of God's testimony (v. 10), and that the divine testimony is for the life of humanity which can only be gained through "having" the Son (which for our author means accepting the creed that the Son was a human person). The course of the logic moves to the source of all truth—God.

9—Now the author argues that, if human witness is admissible, then divine witness cannot be denied. **Receive** means to accept as true. Should we ask what human testimony the author has in mind? Perhaps not, for it is the general principle upon which he is arguing: **The testimony of men** is accepted as a matter of course. Upon this both the readers and the separatists doubtless agree. But surely, then, **the testimony of God** is even more acceptable. The logic is that of "from the lesser to the greater." For **greater** cf. 3:20 above. But the clincher comes in the next clause, which delimits what the witness of God is. God has testified to **his Son.** (The RSV loses the repetitious appearance of four *martyr*-words ["witness" or "testimony"] in the verse.) The divine testimony referred to may be synonymous with the three witnesses of v. 8 or it may be an additional one. In Johannine parlance the supreme witness of God to Christ occurred in the crucifixion, where paradoxically Jesus is glorified by the Father (e.g., 17:1). It may be that the thought of v. 9 is that none other than God has spoken approval of the human death of Jesus in the cross itself. Hence, behind the three witnesses of the Spirit, water, and blood is the authority of God. They constitute "the testimony of God." The two halves of the verse are connected with another ambiguous *hoti* ("because," "for"), which seems in this case to mean that the **for** clause modifies and gives the content of the previous clause.

10a—If the point of v. 9 is established, it therefore follows that failure to believe in the human death of Christ denies the truth of **God's** declaration concerning **his Son. Believes in** (*ho pisteuōn eis*) is found only in this verse and in v. 13. It is common in the Gospel of John to suggest full, personal trust in Christ or God (e.g., 14:1). But it is doubtful that our author distinguished between the meaning of this construction and "believe that" (*ho pisteuōn hoti*, 5:1) or the simple "believe" with an object (e.g., 3:23, where "in" does not appear in the Greek). For **Son of God** cf. 3:8 above. For our author it carries the implication of the humanity of Jesus. **Has the testimony . . . in himself** suggests appropriating the declaration of **God**, making it a part of one's life.

10b—The opposite is now stated. Not believing in the humanity of Christ is equated with not believing **God.** Furthermore, it makes of God a **liar,** attributing the eschatological evil to God (cf. 2:22 above). The source of truth is taken to be false. The author adds to the growing list of charges against the separatists that they violate the very truthfulness of God. The remainder of the verse repeats for emphasis the thought of rejection and reflects the originally oral nature of the words.

11—**This is** further develops the content of the **testimony** of **God,** this time from the perspective of its benefit for humans. In the Greek clause following **that, eternal life** stands first for emphasis. As to its meaning cf. 1:2 above. Through the glorification of Christ in his human death and through the witnesses (v. 8) to that human life and death, God has declared the divine will for humans—that they should live in relationship with their Creator. With the last of the three clauses in the verse the gift of **life** God intends for humans is tied again to Christ. The point is that the relationship God wants for humanity is associated with one's perspective on Jesus. The separatists claimed to have eternal life for themselves but denied the humanity of the Christ. The author is declaring that there is no access to God's gift except through acknowledgment of Christ's fleshly existence.

12—The thought of the last clause of v. 11 is repeated here in an affirmative/negative parallelism. "The one having **the Son**" (*ho echōn ton huion*) is the author's way of saying "appropriated in faith"—standing in a trusting relationship with Christ. However, it clearly has overtones, as well, of correct doctrine, i.e., of holding a satisfactory view of Christ. **Son of God** here should be defined by v. 6, "he who came by water and blood, Jesus Christ."

The section 5:6-12 constitutes a frontal assault on the separatists and their denial of the humanity of Christ. It insists that the tradition of the gospel is replete with evidence for the real, fleshly life and death of the Messiah, and that the life of the community of believers (through the work of the Spirit) confirms that humanity. As we are in the flesh, so was the one who brought us into relationship with our Creator. The argument is polemical, but its truth is central to the Christian faith and life.

■ Knowing and Doing (A Conclusion?) (5:13-21)

These verses function as an effective conclusion of the document, even though they introduce new themes. While we encounter here many of the concerns that dominate 1 John, the section surprises us with some new motifs for which there is no earlier precedent (e.g., the distinction between "mortal" and "nonmortal" sin in vv. 16-17).

The section is tied to the previous unit once again through the association of words. "Life" and "Son of God" are both used in v. 12, and "eternal life" and "Son of God" in v. 13 bind the unit to what has come before.

Structurally, the unit is built around a dialectic between knowing and doing. The verb "know" (*eidenai, oida*) is used six times in the eight verses. The section begins with what believers know (eternal life, v. 13, and God's attentiveness to prayer, vv. 14-15). Then follows a discussion of intercessory prayer as the doing that arises from knowing (vv. 16-17). The work concludes with the assertion of three things the believers know (freedom from sin, v. 18; their relationship with God and the world's subjection to evil, v. 19; and the understanding of truth that comes with belief, vv. 20-21). Within the last triad of statements (vv. 18-21), doing is interjected in vv. 18 ("does not sin") and 21 ("keep yourselves from idols"). "Eternal life" sets closures around the section, appearing in the first verse (13) and the next to last (20).

The blend of knowing and doing epitomizes the way in which this author continually fluctuates between stirring confidence among the readers and encouraging them to Christian action. Hence, this section illustrates again the author's pastoral style.

The Confidence of Faith (5:13-15)

Two subjects occupy the attention of these verses: The purpose of the writing (v. 13) and the assurance that God hears prayer (vv. 14-15).

13—I write . . . to you repeats the common refrain found throughout the document (e.g., 2:1, 12, 13, 26). The Greek of the remainder of the sentence is rather clumsy: "in order that you may know that life you have eternal to those believing. . . ." The verbs **have** and **believe** are present tense, stressing the condition of the believer now. **Eternal** is separated from **life** by the verb **have**—for emphasis, it would appear. For **eternal life** cf. 1:2 above. For **believe** and **name** cf. 3:23 above. For **Son of God** cf. 3:8 above. The author declares the purpose of his writing with words that imitate John 20:31. To provoke confidence has been one of the author's primary intents, if not the total purpose of the endeavor.

14—For confidence cf. 2:28 above. Confidence arises from the fact that God is attentive to prayer (cf. 3:22 above). **In him** is *pros auton* ("toward him") meaning "in God's presence" (cf. John 1:1). **Him** refers to God, even though the immediate antecedent would be "Son of God." The verse echoes John 14:14-16; 15:16; 16:23-26. There, as here, a condition is imposed upon the promise that God hears and answers prayer. **According to his will** suggests that requests made of God are to conform to God's nature and intent. **Hears** implies that God is attuned to the desires and conditions of humans.

15—This verse does little more than repeat for emphasis the thought of the previous one—a practice common in oral communication. For emphasis the pair **ask/hears** is duplicated in reverse order from v. 14. The number of words repeated in these three verses bears mention. **Have** occurs once in each of the three verses (13, 14, 15). **Ask** appears once in v. 14 and three times in 15. (**The requests** is, literally, "the requests which we have requested.") "In him" in v. 14 reappears as **of him** in v. 15. Language is put to the service of nurture in a skillful way, in order to cultivate assurance.

Doing that Arises from Knowing: An Example (5:16-17)

16—But our author is always concerned to shape behavior as well as nurture confidence. Prayer is for the sake of others in need as well as for its own sake. The example is that of a prayer of forgiveness for a sinful colleague of faith. Christians are surrounded in the community of faith by concerned petitions to God on their behalf. The author's bias toward understanding **sin** as an outward act is evident here (**sees his brother** sinning). For **brother** cf. 2:9-10 above. For **sin** cf. 1:7-8 above.

The distinction between **mortal** (*hamartia pros thanaton*) and **not . . . mortal sin** (*hamartia mē pros thanaton*) is problematic. Interpreters have proposed numerous ways of understanding this surprising distinction (cf. Brown, *Epistles*, pp. 613-618). Believing that the author works in the context of the Johannine tradition, it may be best to take this distinction as a reference to the delineation between **sin** which arises from unbelief and that which arises from human failure within the context of belief. That distinction arose as one of the ways of reading the apparently contradictory statements that the Christian does sin and cannot sin (cf. 1:8 and 3:9 above). For the Johannine Christians unbelief constituted the basic sin which deprives one of the gift of a relationship with God (i.e., "life"). It is unbelief that is "sin which is mortal" in the sense that it leads to the opposite of life, death (*thanatos*). Our author's concern for moral living, however, necessitates that there be a recognition of those acts and attitudes which alienate one from God, even within the context of faith. That sin "is not mortal," i.e., does not lead to death in the spiritual sense. In the context of 1 John one is forced to think that the mortal sinners are, in the mind of the author, the separatists.

The author's propensity for the use of pronouns without clear antecedents blurs the meaning of the verse. Who gives **life** and to whom is it given? Since "life" is always the gift of God, the author probably does not intend that the praying Christian bestows life on the offending colleague. Surely, the thought is that prayers bring about forgiveness of sin and not that life is bestowed upon the praying Christian as a reward.

That the Christian is not to pray for the **sin which is mortal** (i.e., the sin of unbelief) is troublesome. Some would suggest that the clause means little more than, "I am not discussing that subject for now." Or, perhaps, "such cases lay outside the normal sphere of Christian intercession" (Brooke, p. 147). Bultmann may be closer to the truth in saying that the point is only that "intercession on behalf of the sinner has its limitation" (p. 87). Even more to the point may be the fact that the author exhibits a certain hopelessness with regard to the separatists who have mortally offended God and the community. There is then a tragic pathos to the words.

17—**Sin** of any kind, however, is serious. **Wrongdoing** is *adikia* ("unrighteousness" or "injustice"). God is *dikaios* (e.g., 1:9), and hence any *adikia* is an offense against God. The verse guards against any interpretation which would conclude that human injustice can be taken lightly, even though there is a deadly quality to that which denies God in a fundamental way.

What the Children of God Know (5:18-21)

The author has chosen to conclude the work with a fanfare of confidence that uses a trilogy of "knows."

18—For **know** cf. 2:20-21 above. For **born of God** cf. 2:29 above. For **does not sin** cf. 3:9 above. **Keeps him** is ambiguous (cf. Brown, *Epistles*, pp. 620-622, for the range of interpretations). The **he** may refer either to Christ or the Christian. The RSV capitalization of **he** unfortunately implies the former, but, unless the author intends a play on **born of God,** it is surely the Christian to whom the **he** refers. Who then is the "keeper"— God or the Christian? The subject of the verb (*tēreō*) elsewhere in the document is always the believer (2:3,5; 3:22,24; 5:3) which is enough evidence to argue that the thought of the verse has to do with the believers' holding fast to God. The verb is used of obeying the commandments and God's word, but only here of "keeping" God. The logic, however, is clear. In keeping the word and commandments we keep ourselves close to God. The first **him,** therefore, refers to God. The thought is that those who truly have their origin and identity in God are faithful in clinging to God.

In the last clause (**and the evil one . . .**) the **him** shifts antecedents to the Christian. For **evil one** cf. 2:13 above. **Touch** (*haptetai*) is used only here in 1 John (and only at 20:17 in the Gospel of John). Brown shows that the verb is used in the OT and Jewish literature to express the act of **evil** (e.g., Job 2:5; Jud. 3:10; *Epistles,* p. 622). Faithfulness to one's birth in God is the best assurance against the onslaught of the force of evil (cf. 2:13-14 above).

19—Now the gulf between those who have their origin in God (represented in **of God**) and those who do not (represented in **the whole world**) is asserted. For **of God** cf. 4:1 above. For **whole world** cf. 2:2 above. Here **the world** is used in the negative sense of the realm of **evil. Power** translates *keitai* which literally means "to lie" or "recline" and is used metaphorically to refer to the "state" or "condition" of something. The world rests within the realm of evil, due to its faithlessness. The implication is clearly that the separatists owe their origin, not to God, but to the forces opposed to God.

20—For **Son of God has come** cf. 3:8 above. **Understanding** translates *dianoia*, a word used only 12 times in the NT and only here in 1 John. It means "intelligence," "disposition," "plan," or "imagination" (e.g., Col. 1:21). Here the sense is "insight" or "perception," and the thought is that God gives the mental disposition which allows one to find truth for his or her life in Christ. Between **understanding** and **to know** the Greek has *hina,* "in order that." The purpose of the gift is to bring knowledge (*ginōskein*). For **to know** cf. 2:3 above. **Him who is true** is, literally, "the true one" (cf. 2:8 above). "Truth" and "true" functioned in the Johannine community as a description of God and the divine revelation (e.g., John 17:3; 1 John 4:6; 5:7). The title, however, is unique. It refers to God, as the next clause shows.

The theme of confidence continues as the readers are assured that they are **in him who is true.** For the expression **in him** cf. 2:5 above. The relationship with God suggested by the expression **in him** is possible because of the relationship the believers have with **Christ.** For the title, **Son Jesus Christ,** cf. 1:3 above. The Christological import of the fleshly, historical reality of Christ is probably implied here as a distinction between the readers and the separatists.

The author approaches the end of his document with an obscurity typical of his writing. To whom does **this** refer in the last sentence of v. 20? Some argue for God, since it is God who has just been named as "true." Some contend that Christ is intended, since it is he who is the last personal noun mentioned. Dodd maintains that the author is deliberately referring to both (pp. 140-141). It may be that Dodd's view is the best solution, since the second predicate of the sentence (**eternal life**) suggests the gift God makes available in **his Son.** For **eternal life** cf. 1:2. Only in embracing the view that Christ made a real, historical appearance does one gain access to an authentic understanding of God and the benefits given to those in relationship with God.

21—One may feel that the final verse of this document is distracting, for it is the first we have heard of idols. For **little children** cf. 3:1. **Keep** renders *phylaxate*, the only use of this verb in 1 John. It means to "guard," "keep," or "secure." In Johannine parlance it was used of Christ's protection of the disciples (John 17:12), the keeping of Christ's word (12:47), and the keeping of oneself for eternal life (12:25). It is a guarding for the purposes of the ultimately important in life. **Idols** presents a final puzzle. What did the author have in mind? (Again cf. Brown, *Epistles*, pp. 627-628, for a discussion of the vast range of interpretations.)

In keeping with the context it seems our author levels one last blast at the opponents, charging them now with the most serious of offenses against God—idolatry. He regards their infatuation with their own views as a kind of idolatry. They have made idols of their own doctrines and have pursued them with a dogmatism which has split the community. As much as a misfit as this final verse may seem, it is a strikingly profound conclusion. It suggests the dangers inherent in human attempts to claim that a single view alone is truth, which in turn relegates all others to the realm of error. One might wish, of course, that the author had scrutinized his own dogmas in the same light!

This final section brings us to the heart of the contribution of 1 John. There is a confidence which arises from the insight of the gospel—one which stablizes human existence and arms persons against that which is unjust and dehumanizing. But that confidence has always to be viewed in a tension with what is required of one to remain faithful. The gospel announces a gift given without merit or conditions. But that gift requires something of the beneficiary—a "keeping," to use the words of our text. The gift might be surrendered if care to cling to it is not taken.

II JOHN

OUTLINE OF 2 JOHN

In contrast to 1 John, the structures of 2 and 3 John are relatively simple. This is due to the fact that both take the clear form of Hellenistic letters.

I.   Salutation: The Elder to the Elect Lady (1-2)

II. An Apostolic Greeting (3)

III. Thanksgiving (4)

IV. An Exhortation: Love One Another (5-6)

V.   Three Warnings and an Instruction (7-11)

   A. Beware of Deceivers (7)
   B. Examine Yourselves (8)
   C. Guard the Doctrine of Christ (9)
   D. Do Not Welcome Those Who Do Not Abide in the Doctrine (10-11)

VI. Closing (12)

VII. Greetings from Other Christians (13)

COMMENTARY

It is obvious that in this document, unlike 1 John, we are dealing with a letter addressed to a congregation. While the form is different and the author uses a self-designation ("the elder") which is missing in 1 John, the situation in which the author and the readers find themselves is very similar to that of the first epistle. The community addressed here is suffering from a schism not unlike that implied in 1 John (cf. Introduction).

■ The Salutation: The Elder to the Elect Lady (1-2)

The epistle begins with a common feature of Hellenistic correspondence.[21] The salutation identifies the sender and the addressee and is followed by the standard greeting.

1—The author gives us, however, not a personal name but only a title, **the elder.** The word, *presbyteros*, literally means "old man." The term may have been the title of an office in the Johannine community, as it was in the later Pauline churches (e.g., 1 Tim. 5:17). The title has roots in the OT (e.g., Num. 11:16-17, 24-25) and the Jewish practice of the first century, which employed elders in both the Sanhedrin (Matt. 16:21) and synagogues (Luke 7:3). The pattern was imitated to some degree by the early Christians, according to Acts (e.g., chap. 15).[22] The term is used only once in 2 John and once in 3 John (v. 1 of each). In assuming the title the writer claims some authority, as the tone of the letters indicates (e.g., the elder issues a judgment on the nature of the true "doctrine of Christ" in 2 John 9, and 3 John 10 implies that the authority of the writer has been challenged). Most important, perhaps, is the assumption that the author is the recipient and guardian of the tradition on which the community is founded (v. 5).

It is impossible from the available evidence to establish the precise nature of the office of the elder and to discern the structure of the community. That there was a council of elders is impossible to discern from the little evidence afforded us. Nor may we assume that the author is one of the original disciples of Jesus. But it does seem to be the case that the elder represented the tradition of the community and had some prestige as one who preserved that tradition. The picture we glean is that of an esteemed leader of the founding congregation of a region. That congregation has spawned new, smaller groups scattered throughout the region (Brown speaks of them as "house churches," *Epistles*, p. 32). The distance between the mother church and the smaller communities is suggested by the proposed visits of the elder (2 John 12; 3 John 10, 14). The younger churches apparently looked to the leadership of the parent body for guidance, or at least the leader of the latter asserted the prerogative of such.

The elect lady is an image of the church held by the first readers. Unlike Paul, the author elects not to mention the specific location of the church addressed (compare 1 Thess. 1:1). **Elect** is used of Christians elsewhere in the NT (e.g., Matt. 24:22; Rom. 8:33; Titus 1:1), and means those selected from humanity by God to be his people. *Kyria* (**lady**) is the feminine form of *kyrios*, "lord." The range of interpretations of the expression **the elect lady and her children** is discussed at length by Brown (*Epistles*, pp. 652-655). It is likely, however, that it is a metaphorical reference to the congregation of Christians. Feminine images of the church abound in the NT (e.g., Rev. 12:1-2; 2 Cor. 11:1-2; Eph. 5:22-31), and they are expressions of the significance of the feminine dimension of human existence for the early Christians (cf. v. 13 below).

The members of the community are related to the whole body

as **children** are related to their mother—an image of intimacy and dependence. *Teknon* ("child") is one of the expressions used in 1 John for Christians (cf. 3:1 above); it is used three times in 2 John (here and vv. 4 and 13) as well as once in 3 John (v. 4). While the author of 1 John would seem to prefer to use the word for the relationship of Christians with God, the elder invokes the metaphor for the relationship between the Christian and the larger community (cf. 3 John 4 below for an exception). The church is depicted by the use of family metaphors.

The elder now speaks of the community **love** (*agapē*) which encompasses the readers. He first refers to the love the author has for the readers, and then the love of them by all who are, in the author's view, genuine Christians. The statement expresses the enveloping concern of the Christian community, but it also wins the readers' sympathy and postures them favorably toward the author. **I** translates *ego*, which emphasizes the author's personal presence in the letter. **In the truth** means for the elder the revelation of God in Christ—the gospel. Although the Greek lacks the definite article (**the,** which the RSV adds) and could be taken to mean "sincerely," "truth" in the Johannine tradition carries theological weight. The elder, however, understands that revelation to be comprised of certain doctrines. Hence, "in truth" means "within the context of a properly understood revelation of God" (cf. 1 John 1:6 above and vv. 7 and 9 below). **All who know the truth** means the whole body of faithful Christians. For the significance of **know** in Johannine usage cf. 1 John 2:3 above.

2—**Because** renders *dia*, "through" or "by means of." The love of which the elder speaks emerges from the **truth.** Love is the direct result of the relationship with God made possible by the revelation in Christ. For **abides in us** cf. 1 John 2:6, 10 above. The expression has to do with intimacy with God as a benefit of Christ. **Will be with us for ever** is literally "is with us into the age." Again the relationship with God is stressed and now its continuing effects (cf. 1 John 2:17 above). The promise of the Johannine Jesus is that the presence of God is never withdrawn from the believer (John 14:16-17).

■ An Apostolic Greeting (3)

Paul begins many of his letters with the greeting of one commissioned to be sent as an ambassador of Christ (e.g., Rom. 1:7). Some such greeting is part of the common introduction of a Hellenistic letter. The elder uses a peculiar form of such a greeting.

Grace, mercy, and peace (*charis eleos eirēnē*) are a unique combination of nouns in the greetings of the letters of the NT. Paul most often uses "grace and peace" (e.g., 1 Cor. 1:3; 2 Cor. 1:2; Gal. 1:3). The three combined as they are here are found in 1 Tim. 1:2 and 2 Tim. 1:2. *Mercy* is found in a Pauline benediction linked with *peace* (Gal. 6:16), and Jude combines *mercy, peace,* and *love* in its greeting (v. 2; cf. Num. 6:25-26). **Grace** and **mercy** are relatively rare words in the Johannine corpus. **Mercy** is found only here and **grace** only here and John 1:14, 16, and 17. **Peace** is used only here in the Johannine epistles and six times in the gospel (14:27 [twice]; 16:33; 20:19, 21, 26). Obviously the elder has been influenced by commonplace Christian greetings and has not drawn the terms primarily from Johannine language. **Grace** represents the free gifts of God to humans, **mercy** the unmerited goodness of God and the restraint of strict justice, and **peace** the condition of one in relationship with God.

The elder's greeting is unique in that it declares a promise—**will be with us** (compare the usual Pauline greeting, which is an extension of his personal greeting to his readers, e.g., Philemon 3). The mention of God and Christ in NT epistolary greetings is common (e.g., 2 Thess. 1:2; Phil. 1:2). **Father** (*patros*) is the most frequent title for God in Johannine literature (cf. 1 John 1:2 above). But the combination **God the Father** is found only here and John 6:27 (cf. John 20:17). The elder again exhibits the influence of other Christian greetings, since the combination is not infrequent (e.g., Gal. 1:3; 1 Thess. 1:1; Jude 1). For the implication of the title **Jesus Christ** in the Johannine epistles cf. 1 John 4:2 above. **Son** is the favorite Johannine title for **Christ** (cf. 1 John 1:3 above), and **Father's Son** an appropriate Johannine construction. It is difficult to know exactly how **in truth and love** are related to the thought of the greeting. Perhaps the author's intention is to say that the truth and love mentioned in vv. 1-2 are the means by which the blessings of grace, mercy, and peace are present among the readers. Through the relationship established in the Christ revelation and within the context of a community of mutual concern God bestows divine gifts. The greeting has the effect of giving the readers confidence amid the troubling circumstances in which they live.

■ Thanksgiving (4)

The epistolary form often includes the author's expression of gratitude for the readers and their faith (e.g., Phil. 1:3-11; Col. 1:3-14).

Rejoiced (*echarēn*) stands for the joy often expressed in the opening of NT letters (e.g., James 1:1; 1 Peter 1:8; Phil. 1:4). The theme of rejoicing and joy are common in Johannine literature (e.g., John 14:28; 15:11; 16:22; and cf. 1 John 1:4 above). Here it verbalizes the intracommunity concern the author feels. **Some of your children** is literally "from among your children" (*ek ton teknon*). **Some** signals the first indication of problems among the readers, for the elder is not pleased with *all* the members of their church. If this is so, the author does not reserve his criticism of some of the members of the community for later, as is the custom in the epistolary thanksgiving (cf. Galatians, where Paul omits the thanksgiving entirely).

Following the truth (*peripatountas en alētheia*) means faithfully adhering to the Christian way, as the elder understands it. "Walking" is a more literal rendering of *peripatein* and is an OT image for faithfulness (e.g., Deut. 13:14; cf. 1 John 1:6 above). The elder employs this image frequently (2 John 6; 3 John 3,4). It implies the living of the faith in behavior, but also—more important here—the profession of a proper doctrinal understanding of the gospel. For **truth** cf. v. 1 above. Now the elder invokes divine sanction for his position. **We have been commanded** is more exactly, "the commandment we have received" (*entolēn elabomen*). The author is speaking of the tradition passed on to the community (cf. 1 John 1:1-3 above). **We** suggests that the readers share this tradition and hence are faithful to it as they share the writer's views. For **commandment** cf. 1 John 2:3 and 3:23 above. **Commandment** here represents the double obligation mentioned in 1 John 3:23 to hold a proper view of Christ and to love others (cf. below). The elder's claim, then, is that by fulfilling these two obligations one "walks in the **truth**."

The polemic and apologetic tone of the letter is set in this thanksgiving, although only by implication. There are those among the readers' community who have parted company with others whom the elder regards as the true followers of Christ. The dimensions of fracture are hinted at in the allusion to the double commandment of 1 John. It is doctrinal (Christological) and moral (failure to love others).

■ An Exhortation: Love One Another (5-6)

The moral dispute among the readers' community is the first issue addressed. The elder makes a plea for mutual love and tries to bolster it with the authority of the community's tradition. The structure of the verses is enlightening:

THE EXHORTATORY INTRODUCTION: "I beg you"
    [The sanction of tradition: Not a new commandment but
    one "*from the beginning*"].
THE EXHORTATION: "Love one another."
THE CLARIFICATION:
    a. "This is love"—"follow his commandments."
    b. "This is the commandment"—
      [the sanction of tradition:
      "as you have heard it from *the beginning*"]—
                      "follow love."

Two observations are called for: First, the circular argument
equates "commandment(s)" and "love." The elder does little to
give substance to these two terms. Second, the invocation of
tradition is interspersed in two places in the midst of the argument, repeating the phrase "from the beginning."

5—**Beg** is a strong translation of *erōtō*, which means to request
or ask. The RSV catches the urgency of the plea, but compromises
the authority with which the elder feels he speaks. For **lady** cf.
v. 1 above. For **not as though** . . . **commandment** cf. 1 John 2:7
above. The similarity of the language argues for a common authorship of 1 and 2 John. For **from the beginning** cf. 1 John 1:1
and 2:7. The **beginning** (*archē*) here designates the origin of the
community in the tradition that is rooted in the Johannine Jesus.
For **love one another** cf. 1 John 2:10 and 3:10-11 above. Mutual
concern and care for those of the community of faith was one of
the distinguishing marks of the Johannine church, as the Gospel
of John suggests (e.g., 13:34-35 and 15:12-17).

6—Cf. 1 John 5:3 above. For **follow** cf. v. 4 above. The plural
commandments occurs only here in 2 John, while the singular is
used three times (vv. 4, 5, 6). The author of 1 John uses the plural
more frequently than the singular (e.g., 2:3,4,7). That a distinction between the plural and singular is intended seems unlikely,
and the variation is probably due only to style.

The exhortation alerts us to the elder's view (shared by the
author of 1 John) that the community is troubled by separatists
whose actions demonstrate that they do not "walk in love." It
appears that in the view of the authors of 1 and 2 John the separatists by their act of disrupting the community have failed to
practice love toward their colleagues. That these separatists also
practiced a kind of "lawless" Christianity devoid of moral regu-
lations (cf. 1 John 3:4-10) seems likely.

The substance of the argument is that faithfulness to God con-
sists above all in a caring relationship with others. If the argument
of the elder seems circular, it is because of the conviction that
love lies at the heart of what God wills for the church.

■ Three Warnings and an Instruction (7-11)

This section constitutes the largest part of the body of the letter. It is comprised, first, of a warning about deceivers who propagate false Christological doctrine (v. 7). That leads, second, to a warning that the readers should examine themselves in order that they not fall victim to the false teachings (v. 8). Third, the elder warns against the consequences of embracing the distortion of true doctrine (v. 9). Finally, the author issues an instruction with regard to how those false Christians should be treated (vv. 10-11). The exhortation in vv. 5-6 has treated one of the features of the separatists and their views—they do not practice what the elder regards as true love of the community. Verses 7-11 treat the other feature of the separatist group—they hold a view of Christ which in the eyes of the elder is dangerous.

7—**Deceivers** (*planoi*) is used only here in the Johannine literature (but cf. a comparable use in 1 Tim. 4:1). For the meaning of the word in this epistle cf. 1 John 2:26 above (where the verb, *planaō*, appears). The deception concerning true doctrine may be part of an eschatological scheme embraced by the elder (cf. 1 John 3:4-7 above). **Many** suggests the widespread threat these false believers pose for the readers (cf. 1 John 2:18 and 4:1). **Into the world** indicates their dispersion among the believers. Now the elder describes the nature of the deception. **Acknowledge** (*homologountes*) is better rendered "confess." **The coming of Jesus Christ in the flesh** implies that the deceivers hold a docetic Christology (one that fails to take the humanity of the Messiah seriously)—the same concern found in 1 John (cf. 4:2 above). **Coming,** however, translates a present participle (*erchomenon*) which has been interpreted by some as a reference to the parousia of **Christ** rather than the incarnation. But the parallel with 1 John 4:2 argues for an allusion to the first appearance of Christ. For **flesh** cf. John 1:14. Those who hold such a view of a less than full human appearance of the Messiah are now identified as the **antichrist** (*antichristos;* cf. 1 John 2:18 above). The phenomenon of what the elder takes to be a faulty Christological perspective constitutes evidence of the final assault of evil in the last days.

8—The second warning calls on the readers to examine themselves. **Look to yourselves** means to see oneself clearly and honestly. **Lose** (*apolesēte*) reminds one of John 3:16 (where "perish" translates the same verb). **Worked for** is also Johannine (e.g., John 6:27; 9:4). **Full reward** fits the future eschatology of the Johannine epistles (cf. Matt. 5:12; Rev. 11:18). Bultmann sees here "a typical Jewish expression" (p. 113), but the idea is far from foreign to the NT. However, it is troubling in that the verse seems to imply a "works righteousness." Interpreters would be less than honest if they did not recognize that the elder does imply such a view. Still, in Johannine parlance the authentic acceptance of Christ is treated as a "work" (e.g., John 6:29), and the term *work* should not be read in Johannine literature with the same meaning Paul assigns it (e.g., Rom. 3:20-28). **Worked for** in the elder's language means to have nurtured one's trust and faith. Unlike Paul, the elder is not attempting to address the relationship between works and faith.

9a—The third warning (vv. 9-11) addresses the importance of true **doctrine**. **Goes ahead** translates *proagōn*, the only appearance of this verb in Johannine literature. Here it means "to go too far" or "to go farther than one should" (Haas, De Jonge, and Swellengrebel, p. 146), and Brown renders it "so 'progressive' " (*Epistles*, p. 673). **Abide in** translates the famous Johannine *menein*. For its meaning cf. 1 John 2:6, 10. In this case it has as its object, not a person, but a **doctrine** (contrast John 15:4). Such a transposition of the language of the Gospel of John is already hinted at in 1 John (e.g., 2:14). **The doctrine of Christ** (*tē didachē tou christou*) can also be translated, "the teaching of Christ." *Didachē* is used three times in the Gospel of John for the teachings of Jesus (7:16, 17; 18:19). Does the expression mean "teachings about Christ" (an objective genitive) or "teachings from Christ" (a subjective genitive)? Given the concern for proper Christological belief in v. 7, the former seems more likely. What the elder surely means is the proper belief regarding the incarnation—Christ's full humanity. Proper doctrine emerges in the discussion with the separatists as a matter of utmost importance.

For **does not have God** cf. 1 John 2:23. A false Christology deprives one of a relationship with God.

9b—In antithetical parallelism the elder restates the first part of the verse now in a positive way. To believe properly brings one into a right relationship with both God and Christ. For **Son** cf. v. 3 above. Here we see the affirmation of the role of doctrine in the life of faith. Authentic Christian trust must articulate itself in a sound way—theology arises naturally from faith itself and informs faith. But we also see the tendency of the late NT church to move toward true doctrine as the safeguard against misunderstandings. Just as official leadership developed to protect the church from being misguided (e.g., 1 Tim. 3), so too did definition of proper doctrine (e.g., Titus 2:1). In the process, something of the dynamic quality of faith as trust is lost when it is reduced to sound doctrine.[23] Second John is an example of how disruption in the community by those who teach a different view than others drives the church to delineate and propagate "true" as opposed to "false" doctrine.

10—Now the elder adds to the three warnings directions as to the treatment of those who teach views which differ from those the "mother church" advocates. When the readers are confronted with one of the separatists (i.e., one who does not teach the proper view of Christ and does not practice communal love), they are to deny that person entry to and the fellowship of the home. **House** (*oikian*) may mean a private home or the house in which the community of faith gathers (cf. Brown, *Epistles*, p. 676). **Give him any greeting** is, literally, "say to him, 'rejoice.'" **Greeting** (*chairein*) signifies the extension of hospitality, and for Christians it would stand for a sharing of a common life in faith. The separatist is, in effect, to be excluded from the fellowship of the church (cf. 2 Cor. 11:4)![24]

11—To share fellowship with the separatists is to become identified with them and their falsity. **Shares** is *koinōnei*, "participating together in a common view." **His wicked work** is, literally, "in his works, the evil (*ponērois*)." "Evil" in the Johannine epistles has the connotation of the eschatological struggle between God and the opposition and the stance of the alienated world over against the Christian (cf. 1 John 3:1-13).

In these warnings and instructions the elder has expressed the profound importance attached to proper doctrine and the dangers posed by improper teachings. There is no room for tolerance when it comes to Christology, thought the elder. This is a life-and-death matter, and one's relationship with God stands or falls on the basis of doctrine.

It is the heat of the battle with the separatists which provokes such intolerance, but it occasions the inescapable question of how conceptuality relates to acceptance of God's revelation. How flexible can the perimeters of Christian belief be without sacrificing the integrity of faith itself?

■ Closing (12)

Like the fourth evangelist the elder ends this letter with an indication that there is much more to say (compare John 20:30). The sentence is, however, garbled (cf. 3 John 13). **Paper** renders *chartou*, "papyrus" (its only use in the NT). **Ink** is literally "black" (*melanos*), used in the neuter to mean "ink," since the black from lamps was mixed with liquid to produce a writing substance. **Face to face** is, literally, "mouth to mouth" (*stoma pros stoma*), an expression unique to this verse in the NT but utilized in the LXX of Moses' relationship with Yahweh (Num. 12:8). **Our** reads "your" in some manuscripts, and the decision between the two is difficult. But in either case, communication with the community has the purpose of bringing **complete joy.** For its meaning cf. 1 John 1:4 and John 15:11.

■ Greetings from Other Christians (13)

For **children** (*tekna*) and **elect** cf. v. 1 above. **Sister** (*adelphēs*) is a variation of "lady" in v. 1 and symbolizes the relationship among the churches in terms of a family relationship. This is a view which arises from the Gospel of John, where the revelation of God in Christ creates a new family of God (e.g., 1:12 and 19:25-27). **Greet you** is a standard conclusion to a Hellenistic letter. The author shifts from the plural pronoun "you" in v. 12 to the singular here, in order to stress the singleness of the community in Christ (i.e., its collective nature).

The message of 2 John was forged within the struggle of a community of faith to preserve itself from dissolution in schism. The author musters all the authority the readers may grant in order to save them from the attractiveness of the separatists' position. The attack is on two fronts: morals and doctrines. Against the separatists the elder asserts the constituting role of community love. That kind of concern for one another is more than a desirable feature of the church; it is the definitive mark of the church. But love must also be linked with proper doctrine. If our heads are confused, our hearts cannot function! For the elder, doctrine is not a mere "academic" issue. It is the steering mechanism which keeps the church from veering off the road. The author may shift the heart of Christianity into the swamp of dogma and lose something precious in the nature of faith. But it is done in an effort to sustain the community and demonstrates that tolerance must finally have its limits, if the church is to have integrity.

III JOHN

OUTLINE OF 3 JOHN

I. Salutation: The Elder to Gaius (1)

II. A Prayer (2)

III. Thanksgiving (3-4)

IV. Two Exhortations (5-11)

    A. Support of and Hospitality for Other Christians (5-10)
       1. The Obligation to Do So (5-8)
       2. Diotrephes—One Who Rejects That Obligation (9-10)
    B. Imitate Good, Not Evil (11)

V. A Commendation: Demetrius (12)

VI. Closing (13-14)

VII. Peace and Greetings (15)

COMMENTARY

Like 2 John, this epistle takes the form of a typical Hellenistic letter (cf. 2 John 1-2 above). In distinction from 2 John, however, it is addressed to an individual instead of a congregation. In keeping with its character as a personal letter 2 John names three persons: Gaius (v. 1), Diotrephes (v. 9), and Demetrius (v. 12).

■ Salutation: The Elder to Gaius (1)

For **the elder** cf. 2 John 1 above. The identity of **Gaius** remains a matter for speculation. It was a common name, appearing five times in the NT and frequently in Roman literature. Two options present themselves: (1) He is a member of the congregation over which the troublesome Diotrephes (cf. v. 9 below) asserts power; or (2) he is a member of a neighboring congregation, and the elder believes that he must warn Gaius of the dangers of Diotrephes' rebellion. The first option is attractive, because it explains the effort of the elder to reassert his influence in the congregation in which Diotrephes has questioned his authority. **Beloved** expresses compassion, but also implies that the author wants to win the receptive ear of the reader, Gaius. The expression is used six times in 1 John (cf., e.g., 2:7 above).

Whom I love in the truth is further evidence of the author's desire to ingratiate himself with the reader (cf. the exact phrase in 2 John 1 above). **In the truth** is within the community of faith, since **truth** is a Johannine expression for the Christian revelation.

Here, too, it probably has the sense of the correct doctrine and posture of Christians.

◼ A Prayer (2)

The thanksgiving section of the epistolary form often includes mention of prayer (e.g., Phil. 1:3-4), and here it is a Christian version of the wish for good **health** found in Hellenistic letters.[25] For **beloved** cf. v. 1 above. **Pray** translates *euchomai*, which is used of prayer to God and of a human desire for something. **All may go well** renders the verb *euodoō*, which means "prosper." **Health** (*hygiainō*) refers to physical well-being and soundness, but in the Pastoral Epistles is sometimes used metaphorically for proper doctrine (e.g., 1 Tim. 1:10). The Greek connects the last clause with the first by means of "as" (*kathōs*), so the author is saying, "may you prosper in **all** ways, as you prosper spiritually." For **soul** (*psychē*), cf. 1 John 3:16. It is used only there and here in the Johannine epistles.

◼ Thanksgiving (3-4)

3—As with 2 John 4 (cf. above) the letter continues with an epistolary thanksgiving in which the author expresses pleasure at the faithfulness of Gaius. For **rejoiced** cf. 2 John 4 above. **Brethren** is a frequent title for Christians in 1 John (cf. 2:9 above) and is used in that sense as well in the Gospel of John (e.g., 20:17). It suggests the family image of the community of faith. It is possible that these "brothers" represent itinerant preachers who moved among the small communities of the Johannine church (cf. 2 John 10). **Truth of your life, as indeed you do follow the truth** is, literally, "your truth, as you in truth walk." For **truth** cf. v. 1 above. It has the sense here both of proper doctrine and appropriate Christian behavior, and its first use in the verse may refer to doctrinal, and the second to ethical propriety. For **follow** (literally, "walk") cf. 1 John 1:6-7 above. It is the ethical properness of Gaius's life the elder will go on to praise (vv. 5-6) and contrast with that of Diotrephes (v. 10). Notice the parallel use of the connective **as,** in this verse and the previous one.

4—The Greek for **greater** is comparative (*meizoteran*), meaning "greater than." For **joy** cf. 1 John 1:4 and 2 John 12 above. For **children** cf. 1 John 3:1 and 2 John 1 above. The **my** (*ema*) is thought by some to be emphatic—"my very own." More interesting is that the author claims spiritual parentage of some Christians, as does Paul, at times with reference to congregations (e.g., 1 Cor. 4:14), and at times with reference to individuals (e.g., 1 Cor. 4:17; cf. 1 Tim. 1:2). In Johannine thought the Christian's parentage lies with God (e.g., John 1:12; 1 John 3:1), and 2 John refers to the readers as children of the church (vv. 1 and 4). Does the elder here refer to those Christians he has brought to faith and who should feel indebted to him, or does the expression claim spiritual parentage by virtue of office? The former is the more likely, since it demonstrates a subtle effort, again, to evoke allegiance from the reader. For **follow** (*peripatounta*) **the truth** cf. v. 3 above.

In the introduction to the letter (vv. 1-4) the author has succeeded in ingratiating himself with the reader through expressions of love and praise, hoping to convince Gaius to accept the elder's authority. But the introduction does express genuine love and appreciation for Gaius. These verses also set the stage for the contrast of Gaius with the rebel, Diotrephes.

■ Two Exhortations (5-11)

The body of the letter is devoted to two exhortations (vv. 5-11) and a commendation (v. 12). The exhortations are of an ethical type, the first having to do with hospitality (vv. 5-10) and the second more generally with imitating good (v. 11). Hence, the concern of the letter is not with doctrine (as is the case with 2 John) but with proper behavior. Both exhortations utilize a contrast. In the first, the contrast is between Gaius's hospitality (vv.

5-8) and Diotrephes' inhospitality (vv. 9-10). In the second, it is between imitating good and being "of God," on the one hand, and imitating evil and having "not seen God," on the other.

5—The setting for the hospitality alluded to here is probably the itinerant preachers who traveled among the smaller Johannine communities. We cannot exclude the possibility that those itinerants included prophets from other Christian churches.[26] Reception of other Christians is a widely attested practice (e.g., Acts 15:4; cf. note 24). For **beloved** cf. v. 2 above. The Greek rendered, **it is a loyal thing . . . service,** is, literally, "you are faithful in doing whatever you work." Hospitality is an act of true faith (*piston,* **loyal thing**), of "faith acting in love" (Gal. 5:6). **Service** means an act which expresses faith (cf. 2 John 8 above). The "work" demanded of humans in the Gospel of John has the sense of believing (e.g., 6:29), but in 1 John is clearly moral behavior (e.g., 3:18, translated "deed"). For **brethren** who **testified** cf. v. 3 above. **Especially strangers** is, literally, "and this [these] strangers" (*kai touto xenous;* cf. Matt. 25:35,38). The "foreigners" in this case may, indeed, suggest itinerants from beyond the wider Johannine community.

6a—Some of those to whom Gaius has offered hospitality have reported it to what appears to be the "mother **church**" of the Johannine community. In v. 3 these traveling Christians have "testified to the truth of your life." Here they **testified to your love,** suggesting the importance of communal love in the concept of truth. **Church** (*ekklēsia*) is here used for the first time in the Johannine corpus, and will appear in vv. 9 and 10 below. Its appearance attests to the influence of other Christian bodies upon the Johannine community. Since there is no precedent for its use in the Johannine materials as a reference to the whole body of believers, it is better to take it as denoting a specific, local community. It is most likely that it refers to the elder's community, although there are those who contend that it refers to that of Gaius (and perhaps Diotrephes).

6b—This clause is, literally, "whom you do kindly sending them forward worthily of God." Notice the repetition of the verb

do (*poieō*) here and in the previous verse—an emphasis upon action. Brown suggests that **send** (*propempsas*) "has almost a technical sense of providing missionaries with supplies that would enable them to journey to the next stop" (*Epistles*, p. 711). It is not clear whether **as befits God's service** modifies Gaius's action or that of those whom he has welcomed.

7—This verse describes the itinerant preachers. Again the literal translation proves enlightening: "On behalf of the name they went forth, taking nothing from the Gentiles." For the use of "name" (**his sake**) cf. 1 John 2:12 above. Whether it is God or Christ for whom "name" stands here makes little difference, in the language of the Johannine epistles. **Set out** (*exēlthon*) summarizes the missionary enterprise. **Heathen** translates *ethnikos*, better rendered "Gentiles." It is used only here and in Matthew (e.g., 5:47—always in a derogatory context). Here it means "non-Christians." The image is that of the itinerants traveling about without possessions and gaining the necessities for life from other Christians (cf. Luke 10:4). It is a mark of faithfulness, apparently, not to beg from or receive gifts from those outside the Christian family.

8—Now the exhortation itself. For **ought** cf. 1 John 2:6; 3:16; and 4:11 above. **Support** (*hypolambanein*) is, more properly, "receive." It replies to the use of *lambanō* ("accept") in the previous verse. **Fellow workers** (*synergoi*) **in the truth** means that by supporting the itinerants one cooperates and is identified with their efforts. **Truth** (*alētheia*) would seem to have some of its original Johannine meaning of the revelation of God in Christ. A basic theme in this verse is the idea that human actions affiliate one with dualistic, cosmic divisions—good or evil (cf. 1 John 3:7).

9a—Attention now shifts from the positive witness of Gaius to its contrast, that of Diotrephes. The first clause suggests that the elder has in the past addressed a letter to the **church** (cf. v. 6 above) of which **Diotrephes** is a member. (**Have written** is an aorist—*egrapsa*.) Speculation as to the identity of this **something** that was written abounds—was it one of the other Johannine epistles or an unknown piece? The latter is the case, since there

is nothing to tie either 1 or 2 John closely to the situation implied
here.

9b—Diotrephes means "nurtured by God," but what we can
know of this figure must be squeezed from these few verses. In
this verse two bits of information are given: First, he **likes to put
himself first.** One is tempted to find a note of sarcasm in the title
the elder assigns Diotrephes—*philoprōteuōn,* "a lover of top dog
status" (the word is not found elsewhere in Greek literature).
Bultmann even sees a play on the title "bishop," *episkopos* (p.
100). Whether Diotrephes held an official position or was simply
a member of the community, he loved power and had a good
deal of it, as the following verses show. Second, Diotrephes **does
not acknowledge my authority,** which in the Greek is literally,
"does not receive [or 'recognize' *(epidechetai)*] us." In the context
of this verse the verb may mean simply that the elder's correspondence with Diotrephes' church has been ignored by him.
Actually what **authority** the elder had is not clear. Was it that of
his formal office, or that of a revered preacher/prophet?

A related question is whether or not Diotrephes was one of
the separatists attacked in 1 and 2 John. It is tempting to make
such an identification, but the evidence is too slim. He is not
accused of any of the doctrinal distortions attributed to the separatists elsewhere. He is guilty of the moral position of the separatists, as we are able to discern it, only in that he does not
extend hospitality to other Christians (v. 10). That inhospitality
may, of course, constitute not loving other Christians (cf. 1 John
4:20-21). It is more feasible, however, to assume that he was no
more than a powerful figure, who was confused by the schism in
the community and had decided to welcome none of the itinerants. In the midst of the controversy he advocated "a plague
on both their houses," and worked to isolate his church from the
others as a way of avoiding becoming enmeshed in the struggle
between the factions. The exact truth evades even our best historical detectives, however.

10a—If *(ean)* may introduce a hypothetical situation, or may
be rendered "when" (cf. v. 14). The implication is that the church

visit anticipated here and in v. 14 is to the community in which both Gaius and Diotrephes are located. **Bring up** translates *hypomnēsō*—"remind" or "call to mind." **What he is doing** is similar to the expression used of Gaius in v. 5 (cf. above) and enforces the contrast between the two figures. The verb **prating** (*phlyarōn*) is found only here in the NT, and means to "gossip," "talk nonsense," or "bring charges." Compare **evil words** with the "evil deeds" of 1 John 3:12 (cf. above).

10b—Three additional charges against Diotrephes are now itemized. First, **he refuses himself to welcome the brethren.** On **welcome** cf. v. 9b above. On **brethren** cf. v. 3 above. Second, he prevents others from practicing hospitality. **Stops** is *kōlyei*, used only here in the Johannine corpus. **Those who want to welcome them** translates *boulomenous*, "the ones who intend." Finally, he is charged with expelling from **the church** (the third use of *ekklēsia*; cf. v. 5 above) those who try to extend hospitality. **Puts out** (*ekballei*) renders the same verb used in John 6:37 of God's refusal to cast out anyone who comes to Christ and in 9:34 of the casting out of the healed blind man (a veiled allusion to the casting out of the Christians from the synagogue). The verbs used of Diotrephes in v. 10 are all in the present tense, which suggests that these are typical and repeated actions. These charges increase the evidence for the proposal that Diotrephes was an official leader in the congregation with the powers of excommunication (cf. Bultmann, p. 101). However, it is just as likely that his power was unofficial and that he was the leader of community efforts to purge his congregation of those who would get the church involved in the schism.

What do we learn of Diotrephes in vv. 9 and 10? (1) He loves prime positions of power (v. 9). (2) He does not receive the elder (v. 9). (3) He gossips with evil words about the elder (v. 10). (4) He does not welcome other Christians into his community (v. 10). (5) He stops others from doing so (v. 10). (6) He puts out of the church those who try to offer hospitality (v. 10). In all of this we gain the impression of a powerful person, intent on preserving the unity of his community. Unfortunately, however, our only knowledge of him comes from one with whom his power clashes.

Verses 5-10 are a skillfully crafted contrast of one who practices hospitality and one who does not. The exhortation to support other Christians is given power by embodying positive (Gaius) and negative (Diotrephes) models. The elder was skilled not only in winning a favorable ear from his reader (vv. 1-4) but also in giving his injunctions the power of specific representations.

11—The second exhortation is to **imitate,** not **evil,** but **good.** For **beloved** cf. v. 5 above. **Imitate** (*mimou*) is used only here in the Johannine literature (but cf. Heb. 13:7). The **evil/good** contrast is also unparalleled in Johannine literature. The order is a clever reversal of the order of the positive and negative models presented in vv. 5-10, and provides continuity with the model of evil in Diotrephes (v. 10) and the model of good in Demetrius (v. 12). The author may be citing a proverb, but it is immediately baptized with Johannine meaning. **Does good** (*agathopoiōn*) is not a Johannine expression (but cf. 1 Peter 2:15) yet sounds in harmony with 1 John 4:7 and 20. For **is of God** cf. 1 John 4:2 above. **Does evil** (*kakopoiōn*) is likewise not a Johannine word (but cf. 1 Peter 3:17), yet harmonizes with 1 John 3:10. For **has not seen God** cf. 1 John 3:6 above. The attention to doing corresponds to the strong ethical motif of 1 and 2 John, in which ethical behavior is viewed as a necessary ingredient of Christian life.

The two exhortations have emphasized the role of ethics in the Christian community. In this case, the elder has moved from the concrete (Gaius contrasted with Diotrephes) to the abstract (imitate good, not evil), suggesting the way in which the inductive is more powerful in moral teaching than the deductive.

■ A Commendation: Demetrius (12)

Another mysterious person steps on stage: **Demetrius.** This is a common name in the Greco-Roman world, but no success has been achieved in fixing the identity of this person, although speculation abounds. It would appear that this recommendation for Demetrius is connected with the elder's attempt to assert some influence in the congregation of Diotrephes (and perhaps Gaius). Connected as it is with the hope of the elder's forthcoming visit to the region (v. 14), it may be that Demetrius is the elder's "front man" (whose task it was to prepare the congregation for the elder's visit), and it may also be that it is Demetrius who is to deliver this letter to its recipient. This commendation may parallel those we find in some other NT correspondence (e.g., Rom. 16:1; 1 Cor. 16:10; Col. 4:7). Some unanswerable questions include whether Demetrius is to replace Diotrephes, whether Demetrius is one of the itinerants discussed earlier, and whether he is to examine Diotrephes for possible separatist leanings.

Demetrius has **testimony** from three sources: **every one, the truth,** and the elder. **Testimony** (*memartyrētai*, literally, "has been testified to") means endorsement, probably in terms of his faithfulness to the Johannine tradition (over against that of the separatists). The need for such betrays the plight of suspicion and uncertainty among the churches (the likely cause of Diotrephes' exclusionary practices). **From every one** means the general Johannine community. For **truth** cf. v. 1 above. Here it may carry some doctrinal overtones, meaning Demetrius subscribes to the views of the elder. As if to climax this parade of endorsements, the elder names himself as a supporter of Demetrius. **You know my testimony is true** may be the elder's appeal to his role as a guarantor of the tradition or as a high officeholder in the community or, more simply, to the credibility he believes he has with Gaius. Demetrius comes, then, with the highest credentials the elder can muster for him.

■ Closing (13-14)

These verses are remarkably similar to 2 John 12, which may indicate one of two things: (1) The same author has used a stereotypical conclusion, varying it only slightly or (2) the verses are from the hand of an imitator (cf. John 21:25, compared with 20:30). The former is the more likely.

Cf. 2 John 12 above. **Had much to write** speaks of the action in the past by assuming the position of the reader for whom the writing was an event in the past. **Soon** (*eutheōs*) in v. 14 is unique when compared with 2 John 12 and may be taken as an indication of the urgency the elder feels about the situation. The author believes that personal **face to face** conversation will ease the crisis.

■ Peace and Greetings (15)

The epistolary form is continued with the simple offering of **peace** (cf. 2 John 3 above). For examples of the use of **peace** as a closing benediction, cf. Gal. 6:16; 2 Cor. 13:11; Eph. 6:23. For **greet** cf. 2 John 13. **The friends** (*hoi philoi*) may indicate personal friends, or it may be a designation for members of the Johannine community. Since Jesus names his disciples "friends" in John 15:14-15, it may be a cipher for Johannine Christians. "Friends, therefore, seems to be similar in meaning to brothers (vv. 3, 5, 10), children (2 John 1, 13), or beloved (vv. 1, 2, 5, 11)" (Culpepper, p. 138). **Every one of them** conceals a nuance of the Greek, which reads, "by name" (*kat' onoma*). This suggests that the elder knows Gaius's congregation rather well, and it is in that context of concern that the letter has been written.

Third John lacks the theological interest of either 1 or 2 John. But its significant contribution is its emphasis on the necessity of *hospitality* among Christians. If our view of the situation addressed in this letter is correct, the elder is saying that isolation and aloofness are not viable Christian responses to a confusing and frightening crisis in the church. Christian love means the extension of hospitality and acceptance to others, even when their presence may involve risk and endanger our peace and quiet![27]

NOTES

1. Only in the late second century do we find 1 and 2 John explicitly cited and both attributed to the author of the Fourth Gospel, who is called "John the disciple of the Lord" (Irenaeus, *Adversus Haereses*, 1.9.3 and 3.17.5, 8). The Muratorian Canon refers to two epistles by the author of the Fourth Gospel without an indication of which of the three are in mind. Origen in the third century is the first to refer clearly to three epistles (Eusebius, *Ecclesiastical History* 6.25.10), although even there 3 John is not quoted.

   In the fourth century there is evidence that the canonical status of the two shorter epistles was seriously questioned (Eusebius, *History* 3.24.17 and 25.2-3). It appears that some attributed them to John the elder, while holding that the gospel and 1 John were from the hand of John son of Zebedee. Still, by the end of that century 1, 2, and 3 John were widely regarded as the work of the fourth evangelist, as the Synod of Hippo (393) and the Council of Carthage (397) held.

   The grouping of these three writings was, then, a gradual result of the reflection of the early church produced only after laborious effort. It cannot be immediately assumed that they constitute the work of a single author, nor that that author was named John.

2. A full list of the common themes shared by the gospel of John and the epistles is not possible, but the following is representative:
   a. Features of the Gospel of John occurring in 1 John:
   Life (e.g., John 1:4)—1:2; 4:9; 5:11-12, 16.
   Eternal life (e.g., John 3:16)—1:2; 2:25; 3:15; 5:11, 13, 20.
   Light/Darkness (e.g., John 1:5)—1:5; 2:8.
   Truth (e.g., John 8:32)—2:21; 3:18; 5:7.

149

1, 2, 3 John

Father/Son (e.g., John 3:35)—2:22, 23; 4:14.

Son (e.g., John 5:23)—1:7; 2:24; 3:23; 4:9, 10, 14; 5:9, 10, 11, 12, 20.

Abide in (e.g., John 15:5)—2:24, 27, 28; 3:15, 24; 4:13, 15, 16.

Know (e.g., John 7:28)—4:6, 8, 16; 5:20.

World (used in a pejorative way) (e.g., John 15:19)—2:15-17; 3:1, 13.

Overcome the world (e.g., John 16:33)—5:4-5.

Keep his commandments (e.g., John 14:15)—2:3; 5:3.

Love one another (e.g., John 13:34)—3:11, 23; 4:7, 11.

New commandment (e.g., John 13:34)—2:7-8.

Spirit of truth (e.g., John 15:26)—4:6.

Advocate (*paraklētos*) (e.g., John 16:7)—2:1.

Receive what you ask (e.g., John 14:13-14)—3:22; 5:14.

Children of the devil (e.g., John 8:44)—3:10.

b. Features of the Gospel of John occurring in 2 John:

Truth—1, 2, 3, 4.

Abide in—2, 9 (twice).

Father/Son—3, 9.

New commandment—5.

c. Feature of the Gospel of John occurring in 3 John:

Truth—1, 3 (twice), 4, 8, 12.

3. Some concepts found in the epistles which are not represented in the gospel include the following:

a. In 1 John: imminent "last hour" (2:18), expiation (2:1; 4:10), anointing of believers (2:20, 27), lust (2:16-17), antichrist(s) (2:18, 22; 4:3), lawlessness (3:4), false prophets (4:1), spirit of error (4:6), day of judgment (4:17), mortal and nonmortal sins (5:16-17), and ethical considerations (3:4; 4:20).

b. In 2 John: doctrine (9-10), the church as "lady" (1, 5), antichrist (7), deceivers (7), and reward (8).

c. In 3 John: church (6, 9, 10), heathen (7), authority (9)

4. Cf. C. H. Dodd, "The First Epistle of John and the Fourth Gospel," *Bulletin of the John Rylands Library* 21 (1937): 129-156.

5. It is now conceivable that we may hear the voice of the separatists in some of the literature of the library from Nag Hammadi. It is the form of gnosticism known to us through that literature which might best represent the position of the separatists some years after the writing of the Johannine epistles. Cf. James M. Robinson, editor,

The Nag Hammadi Library (New York: Harper and Row, 1977). In a most helpful study John Painter has recently argued that the opponents in 1 John had come into the Johannine community after its break with the synagogue. They were influenced by Hellenistic mystery religions and hence were inclined toward a different interpretation of the Johannine tradition (*New Testament Studies* 32 [1986]: 48-71).

6. For the fascinating but unlikely thesis that the elder of 3 John was one of the separatists and Diotrephes a colleague of the author of 1 John cf. Ernst Käsemann, "Ketzer und Zeuge: Zum johanneischen Verfasserproblem," *Zeitschrift für Theologie und Kirche* 48 (1951): 292-311.

7. The following is a diagrammatic representation of the history of the Johannine community which summarizes the history sketched here:

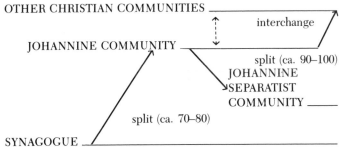

OTHER CHRISTIAN COMMUNITIES

interchange

JOHANNINE COMMUNITY

split (ca. 90–100)
JOHANNINE
SEPARATIST
COMMUNITY

split (ca. 70–80)

SYNAGOGUE

The Johannine community, of course, became part of the catholic Christian church in the second century. We may speculate that the Johannine separatist community (of whose history we know nothing) became aligned with the gnostic churches in the same century.

8. It is ironic that the community charged with distortions and false belief by the synagogue at an early stage in its life should later become the one that levels such charges against a group within its own membership. Bogart speculates about the motives which are expressed in the defense of the parent church in the epistles in relationship to those motives present in the expulsion of the Johannine Christians from the synagogue. For a study of the sociological principles involved in the phenomenon of the struggle for power in a religious community cf. John G. Gager, *Kingdom and Community: The Social*

World of Early Christianity (Englewood Cliffs, N.J.: Prentice-Hall, 1975), especially pp. 79-88.

9. I am using the word "author" throughout the book in the sense of the "implied author," that is, the author as we are able to discern him or her through the document. Likewise, "reader" is used for the construct of the "implied reader." For an introduction to these concepts cf. Edgar V. McKnight, *The Bible and the Reader: An Introduction to Literary Criticism* (Philadelphia: Fortress, 1985), pp. 101-103.

10. I have chosen to use the masculine pronoun for the author of 1 John, but this is not to prejudice the question of the possibility of female authorship. Biblical scholarship, too long dominated by the male mentality, is awakening to the significant role of women in the earliest church, most especially in the Johannine community. Still, given the supposed structure of the church at the time of the writing of the Johannine epistles, it is unlikely that the author would have been a woman. This is in part due to the evidence that the high regard in which the fourth evangelist held women was lost by the time a redactor (possibly the author of 1 John) penned chap. 21 of the gospel (cf. Kysar, *John* on 21:14, p. 316).

11. Cf. C. H. Dodd, *The Interpretation of the Fourth Gospel* (Cambridge: Cambridge University Press, 1953), pp. 201-205.

12. For the various meanings of the word *paraklētos*, cf. Raymond E. Brown, *The Gospel according to John*, The Anchor Bible (New York: Doubleday, 1970), 2:1136-1137.

13. Cf. Robert Kysar, *John, the Maverick Gospel* (Atlanta: John Knox, 1976), pp. 78-79.

14. Cf. the excursus, "Zur Vorgeschichte 'der Antichrist'-Erwartung," in Rudolf Schnackenburg, *Die Johannesbriefe*, Herders Theologischer Kommentar zum Neuen Testament (Freiburg: Herder, 1963), pp. 145-149.

15. On anointing in the gnostic church of a later time cf. R. McL. Wilson, *Gnosis and the New Testament* (Philadelphia: Fortress, 1968), pp. 40 and 70.

16. John H. Elliott has proposed a sociological understanding of the role of the church as a "household" in 1 Peter. In the midst of persecution the solidarity of the community must be established, and it is accomplished with the image of "household" (*A Home for the Homeless: A Sociological Exegesis of 1 Peter* [Philadelphia: Fortress, 1981]). A

similar kind of sociological phenomenon is likely in the Johannine community, where group solidarity against the separatists is nurtured through the image of "family."

17. Cf. the classic discussion of theories of atonement: Gustaf Aulén, *Christus Victor* (London: SPCK, 1953).

18. Victor Furnish has observed concerning 4:21, "This is the only New Testament passage outside the Synoptic Gospels where we can be fairly sure of a direct reference to the Great Commandment with equal stress on each of its parts" (*The Love Command in the New Testament* [Nashville: Abingdon, 1972], p. 151).

19. Furnish proposes that "brother" represents the scope of "neighbor" as it is used in the Synoptic Gospels (*Love Command*, p. 114). Cf. J. A. T. Robinson, *The Priority of John* (London: SCM, 1985), pp. 329-339, for an argument against the exclusiveness of the love command in John and 1 John.

20. Cf. J. A. T. Robinson, "The Destination and Purpose of the Johannine Epistles," *Twelve New Testament Studies*, Studies in Biblical Theology, No. 34 (Naperville, Ill.: Allenson, 1962), pp. 134-138.

21. "No other NT letter, not even Phlm has so completely the form of a Hellenistic private letter as II and III John"; so Werner Georg Kümmel, *Introduction to the New Testament*, trans. Howard Clark Kee, rev. ed. (Nashville: Abingdon, 1975), p. 446. For a discussion of the epistolary form of 2 and 3 John, cf. Robert W. Funk, *Parables and Presence* (Philadelphia: Fortress, 1982), pp. 103-110. Funk argues that the form is an attempt to make the personal presence of the sender real to the reader. For examples of personal letters in the Hellenistic culture, cf. Howard Clark Kee, *The Origins of Christianity: Sources and Documents* (Englewood Cliffs, N. J.: Prentice-Hall, 1973), pp. 262-265. For a bibliography of works on the epistolary form, cf. Brown, *Epistles*, p. 795.

22. Arland J. Hultgren and Roger Aus, *1-2 Timothy, Titus, 2 Thessalonians*, Augsburg Commentary on the New Testament (Minneapolis: Augsburg, 1984), pp. 39-40.

23. For the argument that the Gospel of John anticipates the transition from faith understood as personal trust to faith conceived as proper doctrine cf. Robert Kysar, *John, the Maverick Gospel* (Atlanta: John Knox, 1976), pp. 80-81.

24. The theme of hospitality in the early Christian community is treated in John Koenig, *New Testament Hospitality: Partnership with*

Strangers as Promise and Mission, Overtures to Biblical Theology, No. 18 (Philadelphia: Fortress, 1985). For a discussion of the social dimensions of hospitality among the churches of early Christianity cf. Abraham J. Malherbe, *Social Aspects of Early Christianity*, 2nd ed. (Philadelphia: Fortress, 1983), pp. 60-112.

25. Cf. Apion's letter, in Howard Clark Kee, *The Origins of Christianity*, p. 264.

26. For the phenomenon of itinerant prophets in the early Christian communities cf., among others, Howard Clark Kee, *Christian Origins in Sociological Perspective* (Philadelphia: Westminster, 1980), pp. 68-70; David E. Aune, *Prophecy in Early Christianity* (Grand Rapids: Eerdmans, 1983), pp. 211-217; and Gerd Theissen, *The Social Setting of Pauline Christianity* (Philadelphia: Fortress, 1982), pp. 28-54.

27. Cf. the provocative and ground-breaking sociological study by Bruce J. Malina, "The Received View and What It Cannot Do: III John and Hospitality," *Semeia* 35 (1986): 171-189.

SELECTED BIBLIOGRAPHY

The following volumes are those upon which the author is most dependent and to which references are made throughout the commentary (by author's name and page number).

A. Commentaries:

Brooke, A. E. *A Critical and Exegetical Commentary on the Johannine Epistles*. International Critical Commentary. Edinburgh: T. and T. Clark, 1912. An old but useful commentary on the Greek text.

Brown, Raymond E. *The Epistles of John*. The Anchor Bible, volume 30. Garden City, N.Y.: Doubleday, 1982. Without doubt the best commentary in English, distinguished by its thoroughness and its interpretation of the epistles in the light of the Gospel of John. As do all commentaries since Brown, the present book owes much to this monumental work.

Bultmann, Rudolf. *The Johannine Epistles*. Hermeneia. Philadelphia: Fortress, 1973. A commentary with a strong theological emphasis but marred by the author's idiosyncratic theses, among which is a source proposal for 1 John.

Culpepper, R. Alan. *1 John, 2 John, 3 John*. Knox Preaching Guides. Atlanta: John Knox, 1985. A small commentary, focused on the use of the epistles in preaching; the best of its kind. The approach to the epistles shares much in common with Brown's commentary.

Dodd, C. H. *The Johannine Epistles*. The Moffatt New Testament Commentary. New York: Harper and Brothers, 1946. An important commentary by an insightful scholar, with some attention to the Hellenistic background. Based on the Moffatt translation.

Grayston, Kenneth. *The Johannine Epistles*. The New Century Bible Commentary. Grand Rapids: Wm. B. Eerdmans, 1984. Remarkable for the author's proposal that at least portions of 1 John were written before the Gospel of John.

Houlden, J. L. *The Johannine Epistles*. Harper's New Testament Commentaries. New York: Harper and Row, 1973. A fine commentary, although not as thorough as one might wish. The introduction has useful insights into the relationship of the gospel and the epistles.

Marshall, I. Howard. *The Epistles of John*. The New International Commentary on the New Testament. Grand Rapids: Wm. B. Eerdmans, 1978. An informative commentary written from a somewhat conservative perspective. Use of Greek in footnotes.

Perkins, Pheme. *The Johannine Epistles*. New Testament Message 21. Wilmington: Michael Glazier, revised edition, 1984. Written in a clear style, proposes that much of 1 John originated in preaching. Stresses the rhetorical art of the writing and the sociological setting of the epistles.

Smalley, Stephen S. *1, 2, 3 John*. Word Bible Commentary. Waco, Texas: Word Books, 1984. A commentary second in size and thoroughness only to Brown. Written from a moderate point of view with the most recent bibliographical information on the Epistles.

B. Other Studies:

Bogart, John. *Orthodox and Heretical Perfectionism in the Johannine Community as Evident in the First Epistle of John*. SBL Dissertation Series 33. Missoula, Mont.: Scholars Press, 1977. An attempt to resolve the contradictions in 1 John regarding sin and the Christian. Technical but helpful in relating the gospel and 1 John.

Brown, Raymond E. *The Community of the Beloved Disciple*. New York: Paulist, 1979. A carefully argued discussion of the history of the Johannine community from the time of the "beloved disciple" through the writing of the epistles.

Selected Bibliography

Haas, C., De Jonge, M., and Swellengrebel, J. L. *A Translator's Handbook on the Letters of John.* Helps for Translators. New York: United Bible Societies, 1972. Written in conjunction with the preparation of TEV, with a running commentary on translation problems. Contains helpful information on word meanings, grammar, and structure, as well as other exegetical insights.

Malatesta, Edward. *Interiority and Covenant.* Analecta Biblica 69. Rome: Biblical Institute, 1978. A technical study of "being in" and "abiding in" in 1 John which maintains that the expressions have to do with the interpersonal relationships of the new covenant.

Segovia, Fernando F. *Love Relationships in the Johannine Tradition: Agape/Agapan in I John and the Fourth Gospel.* SBL Dissertation Series 58. Chico, Calif.: Scholars Press, 1982. Argues that the concept of love propagated in 1 John was used to attack docetic opponents and that parts of the farewell discourses of the gospel are from the hand of the author of 1 John and his time.

Whitacre, Rodney A. *Johannine Polemic: The Role of Tradition and Theology.* SBL Dissertation Series 67. Chico, Calif.: Scholars Press, 1982. Compares the polemics in the gospel and 1 John and finds that, although the opponents are different, the methods used are similar in important ways.